Fire on the Water
An Anthology of Black Nova Scotian Writing
Volume 2
Writers of the Renaissance

George Elliott Clarke, Editor

Pottersfield Press, Lawrencetown Beach,
Nova Scotia

© Pottersfield Press 1992

All rights reserved. No part of this publication may be reproduced or transmitted in any form or by any means, electronic or mechanical, including photocopying, or by any information storage or retrieval system, without permission in writing from the publisher.

Canadian Cataloguing in Publication Data

Main entry under title
Fire on the Water Volume 2
ISBN 0-919001-671-8

Includes bibliographical references, Partial contents: v.2 Contemporary writers. 1. Canadian literature (English) — Black authors. * 2. Canadian literature (English) — Nova Scotia — Literary collections. 3. Blacks — Nova Scotia — Literary collections. I. Clarke, George Elliott, 1960 -

PS8235.B55F47 1991   C810.8'96'0716   C91-097610-4
PR9194.5.B55F47 1991

Cover painting: *Moonscape* (1960) by William Lloyd Clarke

Editor's photograph by Andrews-Newton of Ottawa.

This book was produced with the financial assistance of Multiculturalism Canada — The Secretary of State for Multiculturalism and Citizenship.

Pottersfield Press receives block grant funding from the Canada Council and the Nova Scotia Department of Tourism and Culture.

Pottersfield Press
Lawrencetown Beach
RR 2, Porters Lake, Nova Scotia
Canada B0J 2S0

Herin Is Written

Maschil:
Instruction

Dedication 8
Confession 9

Revelation:
Contemporary Africadian Writers

Raymond L. Parker 12
Frederick Ward 15
Alfreda Smith 28
Walter Borden 31
Frank S. Boyd 43
Charles S. Saunders 53
Gloria Wesley-Desmond 66
Maxine Tynes 73
Syliva Hamilton 85
George Boyd 98
Peter A. Bliss Bailey 110
Faith Nolan 118
Delvina E. Bernard 126
David Woods 135
George Elliott Clarke 146
Floyd Kane 159

Selah
Envoy

Lives 164
Acknowledgements 177
About the Editor 178

Maschil:
Instruction

God is the community

*The logo of the African United Baptist Association of Nova Scotia:
(Designer, Henry Bishop, 1991)*

Dedication

To my parents, William, who paints on glass, and Geraldine, who seeks beauty in all things.

To Pearleen Oliver (who guided) and Sylvia Hamilton, the Mothers of the Renaissance.

To Burnley Jones, Walter Borden, and Howard D. McCurdy, MP, the eloquent teachers.

To John Bell, John Fraser, and Charles R. Saunders, who advised and inspired.

To Mayanne Francis, Percy Paris, and Kathleen Tudor, who supported.

To Lesley Choyce, Elizabeth Eve, and Pottersfield Press.

To Anne Johnson, Ramona Hill-Clements, and Henry Bishop of the Black Cultural Centre for Nova Scotia.

To Gwen Whitford, Margaret Campbell, and Barry Cahill of the Public Archives of Nova Scotia (the best archives in the country).

To Tracy Jones of the Halifax North End Memorial Library.

To Gilbert Randall Daye of Maynard Street—and of the Secretary of State.

To David Pigot and Terry Whalen, formerly of the *Atlantic Provinces Book Review*, Harold Marshall of *Caribe*, and Ewart Walters of *The Spectrum*, for publishing the arguments for this anthology.

To Frank Stanley Boyd, Neil V. Rosenberg, James Walker, J. L. Dillard, Grant Gordon, J. A. Mannette, Carrie Best, and the other, *righteous*, pioneer scholars of Africadian culture and history.

To Lorris Elliott, who proved the existence of Black Canadian literature.

To Portia White (1913-1968), my great aunt, who sang a way through the wilderness.

To Terrence Bruce Symonds (1953-1990), who was all we must now strive to be.

To *her*, without whom....

Confession

The text has been divided into four major parts. "Genesis" surveys the writing of the eighteenth and nineteenth centuries; "Psalms and Proverbs" is a selection of oral literature (*orature*); "Acts" presents writers born between 1901 and 1945; and "Revelation" presents those born between 1936 and 1971. The first three sections make up Volume I; the last section appears separately as Volume II.

I have provided notes where necessary, reduced some material, and corrected orthographical and typographical errors. However, in antique texts, I have permitted variant spellings to stand. I have also provided the year of first publication for most of the texts. "1992" marks pieces whose first publication is their inclusion in this volume. Place names are Nova Scotian unless otherwise indicated.

Some writers and works appear here because their presence seemed more necessary than their absence. Generally, I have erred on the side of literary merit rather than cultural representation. Yet, my view of literature is literal—and liberal: I canonize songs and sonnets, histories and homilies.

Even so, some writers and works have been missed for one or both of the following reasons: 1) the lack of opportunity to peruse the minutes of the African United Baptist Association of Nova Scotia and to consult a long record of Africadian newspapers such as *The Atlantic Advocate*, *The Clarion*, *The Ebony [Black] Express*, *The Jet Journal*, *8th of June*, *The Rap*, *Black Horizons*, and *Grasp*; and 2) the lack of community awareness of this project. This compilation is biased, then, in favour of established authors.

Admittedly, this canon is provisional. It is not the last word but the first—a position of some luxury *and* anxiety. If there is a subtle reason for its existence, it is to ensure that Africadians will never again be barred from anthologies of African-Canadian, Atlantic, and Canadian writing in general.

I use the term "Africadian," a word I have minted from "Africa" and "Acadia" (the old name for Nova Scotia and New Brunswick), to denote the Black populations of the Maritimes and especially of Nova Scotia. Other appelations—"Afro-Nova Scotian," "Black Nova Scotian," etc.—are unwieldy. Moreover, if Africadians constitute a *state*, let it be titled *Africadia*.

All faults are mine. However, they are the innocent *faux pas* of an explorer—stumbling, straying, yet, striving to clear and map a path for future seekers to follow.

George Elliott Clarke
Nisan (April) MCMXCII

Revelation:
Contemporary Africadian Writers
1936-1970

Fuss is round
all beautifull
-ness.
—Ward

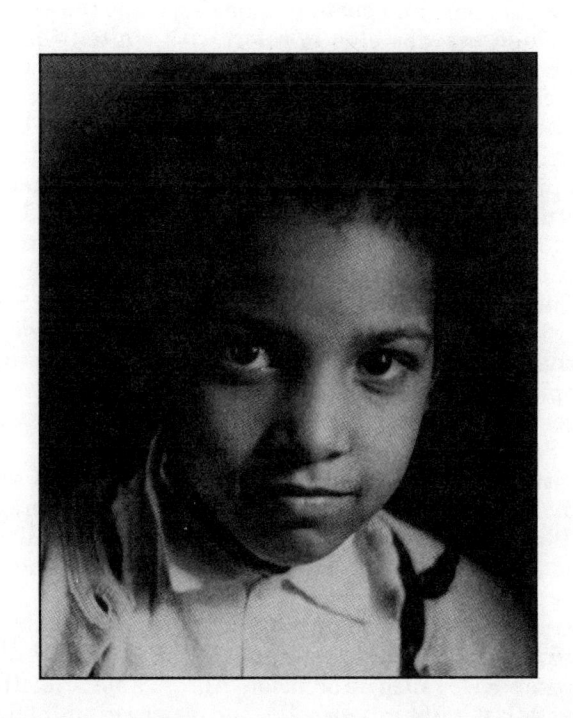

Young girl in Africville, September 14, 1965.
Credit: Ted Grant, Courtesy of National Archives of Canada.

Raymond L. Parker
(1936-)

The Wedding

With help from the women of the village, Sarah made a gown from some of the clothes she had taken from the Fraziers' farm. Taking some away from here and putting some there was the procedure they followed. The dress was blue in color, with white frills around the neck and cuffs around the bottom of the sleeves. The women spent many a stormy night at Sarah's house finishing the dress and also making Abram a suit of clothes for the big ceremony. Abram had no way to purchase a ring; so a silver band was taken from one of the villager's pipes. Sarah's fingers were small and it fit perfectly. The ring was ground down to finger size and polished to a glistening piece of jewelry. Sarah was exceedingly pleased with the ring and could hardly wait for the day when it would be hers to wear for the rest of her life. This certainly wasn't going to be an expensive wedding but the hard work that was put into it and the love that was shared in making the preparations meant more than any wedding the rich white people ever had.

Days seemed to creep by and it seemed that the day would never come for Sarah. But eventually the day did come and they were blessed with a beautiful day. The sun was shining and the weather was warm and the people of the village were up at the crack of dawn making final preparations for the day. Sarah wasn't allowed to see Abram the night before; as a matter of fact, she wasn't allowed to see him before the ceremony began.

The women spent the morning putting Sarah's hair in a fancy hairdo and bathing her and perfuming her with incense, a herb they always preserved for such an occasion. Abram's suit of clothes was far from a tuxedo but it fit him perfectly, and he was proud of the garment made from some of the clothes Isaac had given him. The coat was black in color, the pants were navy blue; and one of the ladies had made him a white shirt from one of her blouses.

By mid-afternoon, the time finally came and the bride and groom were led to the centre of the village to an empty cabin where all their special meetings were held. This was called the Meeting House. Sarah was accompanied by Levi to the front of the room, followed by Charlotte who acted as her bridesmaid. Both Sarah and Charlotte carried bouquets of early spring flowers gathered from the forest.

Levi accompanied Abram to the front of the room, serving as his best man. When everyone got to his or her place, the room became very silent in waiting for the door to open. Minutes passed and then a sound of the beating of a drum was heard, played by one of the men of the village announcing the entrance of their leader. This happened any time there was a meeting of the village or on any special occasion. The door opened and in walked their leader, dressed in a gown made by the village women.

As Willie Thomas walked to the front of the room, the people stood up and began singing their village chant, signifying homage to their leader. When the chant was over they became silent again, waiting for their leader to speak. The drums took up another rhythm now, signifying the beginning of the ceremony.

And then Willie began to speak in a low voice, picking his words carefully. "Men and women of dis village, we's meet here dis afternoon to join two youngins in marriage."

"Amen," said the villagers in one voice.

"Two youngins dat came to our village a few months ago," continued Willie, looking around the room.

"Amen," voiced the villagers again.

"We's all know dat the Laud don't think it fittin to live together without bein married."

"Amen."

"These youngins want to obey the Laud's wishes."

"Amen, Brother, amen."

"So today we's goin to grant them His wishes."

"Amen."

"Do you's Abram Johnson take dis woman Sarah Jackson as yo wife?"

"I's do."

"Do you's Sarah Jackson take dis man Abram Johnson as yo husband."

"I's do."

"As leader of dis village and in da eyes of da Laud, and in the eyes of des people, I's call you's man and wife."

Sarah and Abram faced each other and Abram put the ring that had been made on Sarah's finger, then they embraced one another.

"May da good Laud bless you's both," said Willie, shaking their hands and kissing the bride.

Then all the people began to applaud, shouting, "Amen, amen." Everyone stood in a line to kiss the bride and shake Abram's hand.

When the ceremony was over, women of the village brought in various types of food and placed it on the table and a great feast marked the conclusion of the wedding ceremony. Various gifts were given to the bride and groom, mostly hand-made utensils crafted by the people of the village. After this was over, the people went to their respective homes, leaving Sarah and Abram to be together on their wedding night.

It had been spring for several weeks now and preparation for planting a garden was one of the most important things for each home in the village. Only a few tools were available for the twenty-one houses, so everyone took turns helping his neighbour plant his garden. There were quite a few potatoes left over from the winter months and they were divided evenly for each home owner to plant. Seeds from squash, pumpkin, cucumbers, beans, etc., were saved and dried through the winter months for the following year's gardens.

The soil was rocky; the land was high and so the moisture didn't last for long. The gardens had to be watered at least every two days. When it rained, the gardens didn't need watering and the constant threat of weeds choked the new plants. The villagers worked constantly at their gardens; and when the dry spell came in mid-summer, they had to carry water from long distances. Two or three persons would go with a hand-made drag[1] and carry water in twenty gallon barrels to water their gardens from various springs in the wooded areas.

Abram's donkey served well in this respect, and the neighbours paid Abram by cutting hay in the woods clearings where grass grew. The hay was put in the remaining building that was never used and the donkey was kept there too in the winter months. Wild oats grew in the forest and this too was cut and given to Abram for his most essential beast.

1987

Note
1. A horse-drawn plank-platform on wooden runners.

Frederick Ward
1937-

The Curing Berry

Around 12 Bars in 3/4 Time

I made a
Song with your
Name.

Sort of
Whined it and
Cried it   I made a
Song with your
Name — and when I
Sighed it, I
Put a spell be-
Side it what made a
Song.

I made a
Song with your
Name.

I wore your
Dress and apron in your
Step   I made a
Song with your
Name — and when I
Tried it, I
Bowed and hid my eyes to
Hide it what made a
Song.

I made a
Song with your
Name.

Tried to de-
Fine it   I

FIRE ON THE WATER

Pined it   I made a
Song with your
Name — it bore your
Wrist lace and knitted
Charm tied about your
Face what made a
Song.

                                                1983

Who

Who gonna bargain for my soul
Who gonna bargain last

Her mouth stretched
withered and flush:
the crimson what come'd
round a bruise

though the voice
be a high sparrow-chirping:
the sudden flutter-ups-of-a-
startled thing

When she gripped a lone note
a breeze neath silk
be of report
and carried the thought of a

modest young girl
stooped to press her apron
gainst her dress
ironing it from the heat of her thighs

then standing erect
—surrounded by ancient
yet courageous tremblings.
shouts:

Who gonna bargain for my soul
Who gonna bargain last

                                                1983

FREDERICK WARD

From: Who All Was There

Mary

Most I have were my fears and a hatchet when I
crossed over into Canada...I took my first night
in liberty high on a tree branch next of...all
as I could tell, a bird in shivers with its head
hid mongst a wing...I hummed to it to calm our
fears...give me confidence that the bird ain't
fly away during the night...be a sign to me,
owning up to my being human, that even not some-
thing shivering next to me I could consider with
a friendliness. Am I human. They never give me a
good characteristic to go on. Even my songs be
filled with the guilt grafted onto my soul. I
wanted to touch the bird but to do that I haves
to let go the branch and I'd lose my hold to it
cause my other hand grasped my hatchet.

The Lord do send us some tests, don't He? Break-
fast be one of them. In the middle of my pity for
the bird...sunrise on my soul! I got hungry.
Since the bird's head were still neath its wing,
it had no head...I considered it cooked like the
fowl I served in bondage...and since it continued
to shiver. I thought what a mercy I'd bring to it.

But had not this been the lie what got me here:
were I not dead cause I possessed no tongue under-
stood...were it even not a mercy, a right to beat
me cause I shivered with fear...have I not used it
gainst my own for proof? Am I mad? I am split
from my most confident self-assumption...yet the
Lord send a grace in some stranger's hand: a prayer
and a epistle...set my mind in *'the possibility'*
what changed the quality of my thought...kept it
safe whilst I seen them go crazy with their makings;
realized a spirit in me not noticeable as they checked
my teeth...snatched what be theirs from tween
my legs to beat on and chew on it...

The bird flown away...left its shiverings on the
branch and I climbed down into snow.

1983

FIRE ON THE WATER

Blind Man's Blues

The best thing in my life
was a woman named Tjose.

We never had to sneak for nothing
strong woman.

Put you in mind of a lone bird at dawn
standing without panic in the dew.

She kissed me so hard
she'd suck a hum from me

The best thing happen to her
were my own papa.

I found her
he had more experience

I think the hound in me sniffed out something—
something about her

And I caught her sucking that same hum from him.
I went dumb staring...and she seen it.

My to God, she tried to wave me off–
Papa say:
      —O son
       O son

And I don't think she wanted me
to look on my naked papa like that

She throw'd lye
in my face.

1983

Dialogue #1
Mama

    S⎯⎯ enough Lord, sometimes I just went and stood in the
    ⎯r...and had me corner. You know the day they come'd-
    room to room I moaned some tween me teeth til moaning
    uiet yelpings be all I had left. Then come'd the

knock. Me fears swelled up in me jaws...stretched the soul
of me to makes fer an explosion tween me lips, yet...

The bulldozer be next door to me friend Miss Chisholm's
place.Tweren't no crash such that would slide into a
child's crying, makes fer you to come running to the
window to see what fer. No! This sound'd keep me pressed
to me corner, covered over on meselfs and come'd to trembling.

I prayed: Please give me me tiny crimes. Fergive me me tiny
crimes. Fill the little emptinesses in me—and Lord bless.
I swear I heard something...a choir singing softly:
"Have faith Adeline!" The knock come'd again. I lurched...
then folded me arms about meself. Most proudly I beckoned:
it's open.

Then shadows come'd right round me. Come'd in here without
asking pardon fer themselfs and took things from they place
whilst I mumbled and pointed.I touched me breath and tried
to slow them to take care. Some one of them apologized fer
moving me. But they made off with me evidence. I ACCEPTS!
But I expects they'd lease done the least, ceptin they ain't.
THEY MOVED ME IN GARBAGE TRUCKS![1]

1983

Dialogue #3
Old Man (to the Squatter)

—Listen here, son. Did you think this were gonna work?
Were you fool enough to think this were gonna work?
They ain't gonna let us put nothing up like that and
leave it. They don't intend to let us git it back. You
ain't a place. Africville is us. When we go to git a
job, what they ask us? Where we from...and if we say
we from Africville, *we are Africville*! And we don't git
no job. It ain't no place, son. It were their purpose to
git rid of us and you believed they done it—could do it!
You think they destroyed something. They ain't. They
took away the place. But it come'd round, though. Now that
culture come'd round. They don't just go out there and
find anybody to talk about Africville, they run find us,
show us off—them that'll still talk, cause we Africville.
NOT-NO-SHACK-ON-NO-KNOLL. That ain't the purpose...fer
whilst your edifice is foregone destroyed, its splinters
will cry out: *We still here*! Think on it, son. You effort

will infix hope in the heart of every peoples. Yet, let's see this thing clearer. If our folk see you in the suit, we may git the idea we can wear it. The suit might fall apart, but son, it be of no notice. We need the example. Now go back...and put you dwelling up again.

1983

Lady Susuma's Dream

There were a great tale Lady Susuma once told. The dawn birds were involved in morning chatterings whilst Lady Susuma lie near woke on her pallet, listening through the open window, not sure she'd past the night...taking no deep breaths. Of a sudden, a marvelous 'Call' come'd over the birds' voices, silencing all and quickening Lady Susuma's heart. She tightened her brow and forced *"the step of crows"* upon her countenance. Again the 'Call' be raised, presenting itself as many voices in one...antara[2]: pan-pipes surrounded with the shrill of the cicada and the chimney swifts' song—many colored singing with its own echo supporting it. Not a lot of chirping and fuss, just a swell of comment with a hint of overtone. Again! It confused Lady Susuma. Were it a dream, she questioned herself. Nothing she'd ever heard afore be the like of this. Surely it sang about the heart, hope and delightsomeness. Her hands played about her mouth with it and in near whispered thought-tones she painted it:

"O! Imagine its plumage."

Head high, a gloriously crested bird!

"Yes. Must be, Lord! that'd create in myself such images as what might do cause me to put some patting upon my breast. Yes, of memorable plumage!"

Shiny blue-blacks with sprinkled tinges
of green and wee-yellow peek-a-boo edge.
A scorch of red: seahorse shaped, hook-
halfway round and back of its eyes, and
curled down its neck.

"It ain't perched."

Mysteriously held to a stance from its breast
noble as the highest aspiration in humankind.
Its long tail feathers, even not in repose, be
a calligraphy of rhythms.

FREDERICK WARD

"SPLENDID SPECIALNESS!"

She shouted it through her imaginings and greeted her 'impressions' in ancientnesses: "Woyi bie! Woyi bie! Welcomewelcome! O Wedo, calling Wedo, O Wedo there, be that you..."

What were left, she mouthed...gripped and hugged at it to herself. The song of her thought bloomed and come'd a nuisance in her...pushed at her till she be forced to arise and seek out the 'Caller', yet the 'Call' be like a hand upon her chest...stayed her movement, oppressed momentarily the struggle in her whilst teasing her imagination to more heights. She thought tween the grunts from her:

Lord, I must see it. Let me up from here,
please, Mercy.

She steadied herself to her knees...then stood, took a deep breath and resolved it toward the window. Lady Susuma raised the shade... Her mouth opened, but not on words...truthful panic gripped her.

What were there were of two sides. That what be on her mind overlay that what she seen; a clothesline of sheets in the breeze being jerked past the corner of the neighbor's house...someone were taking the sheets off the line. Again the 'Call' were raised. Lady Susuma's eyes darted the length of the clothesline over a rusted pulley attached to a tree and crying in pulled spurts...the sound bending near the end of each pull and breaking through a certain resistance to sing:

Rhueee! Rhueee!
Rhueee! Rhueeeeeee!

1983

The Death of Lady Susuma

LIGHTNING were into the river. The weather turned to steel but Lady Susuma set herself gainst it to greet something in it. Her 'voices' were at her, say:

Not to worry bout the 'Robes moving on the leaves'
We brought him come'd for to git you:
Kept Sweet Under the Pressure

When she heard it, she put her palm gainst her mouth then doubled it into a fist...crushed her lips...her hand flowered open afore her face, and she caught-smeared a tear...inside a shiver she done it:

FIRE ON THE WATER

"Yesssss, O Be Jesus, yes."
It were a quick and trembling-tickled 'yes' hushed as through a hollowness neath ovals filled with finger pressings waved off by hen's down, tied at the hollowness's end in streamers...sing a softness.

She squinted out on shadows...choked the sobs in her, says of a memory:

"Sometimes when he be sleeping long...late, and I be feeling a bit alone, I walk to a tipping within myself to his room...pass my shadow across his eyelids...he always stirs his brow, and I imagine I be in his dream. And if he wakes, I be 'home' in his mighty stare: standing with no blouse on, in two pools of pale blue set in soft scottish pink surrounded by an autumn wheat field.

She peered out to see closely...sought him on the path. He started talking to her from down the road, shouting love:

"It's like a four letter word strung across a barn wall, trying to say it happened. DAMN!" He says this in his highland talk, waving,

Ar bidh
Is sinn
Cridhe

Mor
An daimheach

Uidhe agus eadar
A

Ar cridhe bidh mor daimheach
Agus a is an uidhe eadarainn[3]

Lady Susuma gathered herself together as he approached the porch-stoop. He stepped it. He bowed off his hat and she lowered her gaze but he weren't in it. Like a picture she sit, sit in her rocker in the doorway...barefoot, a fistful of hairpins resting on her lap, mostly covered by her other hand: its thumb drying tear-wet and favouring the veins in the fist...tracing them. She always have a little sweater over her draped around her shoulders...says, to keep the chill way from her.

She reach-caught the door frame and pulled herself up...took in a breath, balled it under her cheeks and stepped onto a twisting...she fuss of it in her smile but the hurt set trembling through her lips and neath her talk:

"Morning."
Her mouth pruned it in dignity...says it like a bird do with the 'goodgood!' and a 'mymymy!' in it, the purpose subtle but bent as she sniffed:

"There's more truth in a dead baby's countenance than on your tongue. When you coming back? You always coming back."

She placed the hairpins in a neat pile on the bannister, stepped and twisted to a window box and snatched a brown leaf from a bluish red fuchsia plant...hid it in her fist. She turned with his voice in her ear:

"You been carrying all that round with you?"

She paused:

"Yes, I done."

"I been carrying mine about with me, too."

"What do it all mean to you?"

"What?"

"Everything I just says to you."

"As much as it means to you. I love you, too, you know."

The rest be private. But it seems Lady Susuma drifted awhile...spent it gazing on 'someone' and hugging the bannister post about it...rubbing her cheek gainst it there in the rain. She dropped the leaf...waved a 'go on way from here' but then stretched forth her hand into 'somebody's' grip...gripped, and come'd off the porch dancing. Yes. Dancing. Once you can put your hand on the bush the curing berry be there for you.

                                                                1983

Riverlisp

Purella Munificance

When Grandma Snooks spoken'd you see'd

a sleeping bee
cuddled in a tear drop
hidden hind a elephant's ear

...cause she talked in them parable kind of visions to show her meanings: 'Fuss is round all beautifull-ness. When you's in trouble boy, you just seeks that inner place you got it! we all's got it!'

But Micah Koch's *inner place* was all fuss too. He'd seen Miss Purella Munificance.

Dear sweet Purella Munificance the huckster man on his produce wagon, put light to your meaning so we can understand huckster man be thinking on your continence he sing the painter's brush strokes of your mouth; a low soft soothing: ahhhh sound of the sea bird, leaning on the air! and shout:

'Oooo, tomatoes's red ripe!
Cabbage tender peas from the vine
Sweet...'

and draws them who wish to buy in a voice that forgits what he be selling. The womens is moved, tho. Huckster man be so taken he neglec'd and one woman is put to ask for her change: 'Owe up, what you owe me, man!'

Mr. Makin It, say: 'Yes, you bet. Sit down here with me...I tell you. Purella, could put a thot in your mind like, that what so you'd believe in her werent never gonna be lost or gone! And patient? I members she be waiting three days for a person to show up who promised to come'd over in fifteen mins. No, I dont lies. I be that friend and when I come'd acting out my lies to tell, Purella just sees me and a great sun come'd over her face and she says: "Yeah, at last!"'

He look up at the sky to see if God were looking and take him a good drink lowered the bottle and his head eyes closed squint bove a nose in s'pantion breathing on lips shaped after the raw persimmon touch: 'Oooowhee! I'm gonna git caught one day...' as if the Lord didn't already know'd.

'When Miss Munificance be passing old mens on th street corner falls into th "unpire slouch" position bent over shaking they head under a hand shading they eyes so to see th *strike coming in,* Purella Munificance gonna be home free –if she *just would!*

'O the boys were at her door but usually got shush'd way. Her mama make her wear long skirts and dresses all th time she were growing up and Purella be obedient aint never give her mama a moments bother. The pimps were always after her and th preacher's known for talking pass you in her direction, when she be round. Yet, she treated everyone with respec. She once were heard to say: "Inevitably we is one." She tol, she been dreaming of a great inte-colored parade! and when she dreamt that, she clasp'd her hands and shouted: "WHAT A LOVELY BOWL OF FRUIT…"

'But that aint had no meaning for most and some'd swear the girl were unhappy…

touch me
touch me
O let me see

'…so when Micah Koch come'd to her home to sell his Bibles, I tells so you could understand why, for her, that parade dream come'd real and they says that Micah Koch's heart were taken! and that later, he cried as he were trying to sell a Bible when reading from Solomon and Sheba —Kings 10:1-13.

'No one knowed th moment what it were in which that Micah Koch and Purella Munificance see'd the Lord in each other's face and being. You may think it questioning that I says they see'd th Lord in each other's selfs but the Lord, here means sacrifice—that's Love—and that's what they were ready and looking for to do. SACRIFICE! That, as far as I can says, were it. Sacrifice. No one knowed how they met, but they done. Aint none ever see'd them together, but people talked. Some out of fear some were jealous and others just vicious.

Fuss is round
all beautifull–
ness

'Seems like all th troublin things you could say were cut loose on sweet Miss Purella the childrens would run to her on th streets—laughins—put they fist on they little hips –being in th ways of they mama's—switch dance and sang:

'you got a white man
you got a white man'

25

'...and run way, they tongues jabbin at her. I sure Miss Purella's tears drained backwards directly thru to her heart, cause we who be sitting on th curbs and standing in th doorways never see'd a drop.

*O hound
of the crucible!*

'Put me in mind of Miss Jessups's boy's affair...

'Yes, you bet! many is the swift tongue of elegance to put words so to touch your inness and makes you to thinking on vision pictures of lovers that fill-heat the heart huh, huh! even lovers in hell trying to 'scapes. Micah and Purella werent th difference. What they had was private and maybe that's why people talked made up and put words in they mouths and movements to they bodies over near the Japanese bridge one night. Poor Miss Purella.

'I guess the sweet child come'd to think in th way that the world was gainst her and in th middle one night, she just let a screamed. It took so long for th scream to reach nowheres that they werent no echo. She stop'd somewheres and aint been with us since!'

Makin It took a long drink look off after in the way of some noise: 'You knows, I just worries bout God ketching me with my bottle. I worries lots cause I sleeps with it...'

'Th worst thing in th world is to be goin thru something by yourselfs afore a audience, like people on the street. So Purella let to walking in th streets is always telling what she be going thru and why even to burst into tears in the middle of th street and then stopping a random person and telling them what was happening to her: "I just been membering how daddy died of..." and she'd cry and embarrass the poor person way.

'Caint say what happened inside Micah Koch. He looked the same everyday cept he lost a might bit weight, tho. He didnt not sell many more Bibles, after just hung round.

'Mama Fuchsia—she truely loved that man—went to shushen and put shame in they hearts. She and the church women delicate in they care surrounded and gave assurance to Mr. Koch that everything would be put right if he'd only just come to th Lord come to th church! Took some time but one old Sunday night baptismal night it were up come Mama Fuchsia head high, but humble with Micah Koch. Come'd right in th church and sit if you please, afore th amazement! Rev. More were opening th doors of th church and asked: "Is there a sinner among us? Th Lord ask me to ask." All heads turned to Micah Koch.

Mama Fuchsia leaned his way whispered: "Raise your hand, Honey."
DONE.

'Rev. Mores come out of th pulpit walked up th ile and stood afore Micah: "Th Lord welcomes every soul in th Kingdom. And th Kingdom here on earth is th church. Let's hear you say amens."

(answered) "You, young man been a servant of His for our people with your Bible selling and all. Th Community loves you as their own and what better than you show *your people* what th Lord done tol and we here believes—that all th Messengers is one spirit and loves us cause we is one."

'Micah drop'd his head like to pray. Rev. Mores started to sweat, one stream catching th corner of his lip—left side—in a come-on-sinner give-in smile. Th water in the baptismal pit stood cold and waiting waves rocking like th moaners who now filled th chrch with low chant...

'I likes to thinks on Mama Fuchsia's face brown and beaming bright.

"'Just like the Lord would say it; bless you, Honey
I buys one of them with the pictures.'"

1974

Notes
1. The belongings of the people of Africville were moved by City of Halifax garbage trucks because moving companies refused to do so. Africville, a community which had existed on the south shore of Bedford Basin since 1815, was bulldozed by the City of Halifax in the 1960s and its residents relocated.
2. A Peruvian pan-pipe.
3. Gaelic: Our are / Is us / Hearts // Great / The friends// Space and between / That // Our hearts / Are great friends / and that / Is the space between / Us.

Alfreda Smith
1938-

Two Poems for Children

Nature

As I look across God's beautiful world,
I see the sunshine glow.
I see the beauty of natural things
As the waters drift to and fro.

1992

My Seed Will Grow

When I plant a little seed,
I know that God is there.
I know that He will help me feed
And water it so dear.

I pray that He will send the rain,
To moisten and help it grow.
And when I go to check it out,
I'll be glad to see it glow.

1992

Two Hymns

God Will See Me Through

E-m-m-m-m when I'm in trouble,
God will see me through.
When I need His help, yes,
He will help me through.

Chorus:
He gave me the victory,
Gives His love so tenderly,
When I'm in trouble
God will see me through.

When I'm hungry, He will feed me.
He's my bread and water, coming from on high.[1]
He's the Lily of the Valley,[2] the bright and morning star.[3]
When I'm in trouble, God will see me through.

When I'm lonely, He will comfort me
He's my comforter, a friend indeed.
He takes care of my every need,
And he supplies it all indeed,
'cause my Jesus will always see me through.

1992

I Want to See Jesus

Lord, help me, help me make it to the end,
Lord, help me, for you are my precious friend.
Lord, help me, help me make it to the end.
I want to see Jesus, I want to see Him.

Lord, help me, help me walk from day to day.
Lord, help me, as I walk the narrow way.
Lord, help me, Lord, help me in the narrow way.
I want to see Jesus, I want to see Him.

Chorus:
Because He walks with me, and He talks with me
Along life's narrow way.
He walks with me and He talks with me,
And He keeps me from day to day.
And when my Lord, when I see your blessed face,
I want you to be pleased, be pleased with me.

Lord, help me, just you know what lies ahead.
Lord, help me, yes you give my daily bread.[4]
And when my Lord, when I see your blessed face,
I want you to be pleased, be pleased with me.

Lord, help me, help me praise you constantly.
Lord, I thank you, you're preparing a home for me.
And when my Lord, when I see your blessed face,
I want to see Jesus, I want to see Him.

1992

FIRE ON THE WATER

Notes

1. Revelation 7:16-17.
2. Song 2:1
3. Revelation 22:16.
4. Luke 11:3.

Walter Borden
1942-

Tightrope Time

Vital Statistics

I am Nature's love-child,
And Freedom is my father;
I have been called by many names—
I am called by many still;
But Restless is the name they gave me,
And I am fashioned from the wind.

Born on some forgotten *FRY*day,
That's *FRY*day with a 'y',
Not *FRI*day with an 'i',
At half past discontent,
Mama sat down on life's sidewalk,
Spread her legs
And pushed one ain't-no-problem time;
And spewed me there
Where *MAYBE-YOU-WILL-CHILE BOULEVARD*
Cuts across *MAYBE-YOU-WON'T-CHILE AVENUE*,
And Indifference sauntered by
To serve as midwife,
To wrap me in my soul and say:
You are Nature's love-chile—
And Freedom is your father.
You'll be called by many names...
I *am* called by many still,
But Restless is the name they gave me,
And I am fashioned from the wind...
From the wind...from the wind...

1986

20/20 Vision

Death came riding
over the hill by my house
on one such Saturday afternoon.

FIRE ON THE WATER

I sat on Granddad's step
that faced toward the road,
holding my nickel
and clutching on my dime,
and waited for my cousin
to gather up his treasure.

I watched a frantic, little ant
search diligently for hers
and naughtily,
but never with malice,
I frequently blocked her path
and watched her flee
in many directions—
exasperated.
The ant and I were playing
on each other's frazzled wits
when a happy little boy
with pleasure on his mind,
heard death give out a greeting,
and a machine gone wild
showed the power it had
over man, its creator.

(Discordant strains of *London Bridge*.)[1]

My golden, private Saturday
dissolved
into a grotesque circus
of broken limbs
and blood
and dust
and shouting, screaming mobs
and neighbourhood gossips
who, like maggots
seem, forever, to be drawn
toward the kill,
and then devour in equal measure,
the tragedy
and tidbits of the latest news—
stopping now and then to sob a *MY!
MY! MY! MY! MY!*

I watched the grieving mother
throw herself upon the ground
and wondered why

WALTER BORDEN

she laughed
so high
so loud
so long!

The driver of the car just sat
and sobbed
and shook
as I recall,
and that disturbed me.
I had never seen a grown up man in tears.
His friend just thought of other things;
I could tell by how she stared
and frowned—
and I recall attempting to locate
the object of her interest
that seemed suspended somewhere
off in space...
I've heard it said
she stared like that
for many, many years.

And deep inside,
with sadness all around,
I felt that I should sense
a little sadness too;
and don't you know, I really did.
But somehow it was plain to me
that no one there would understand
my passion for the movies.
I turned from all that misery.

My mother unpacked groceries
when I arrived back home—
they were part of Saturday afternoon—
and as she knelt
among a jungle of paper bags and boxes,
I saw her wipe a tear away
with the corner of her apron.
Something told me I should cry,
so I pressed and rubbed my eyes
until one tiny little drop
escaped...
and trickled down my cheek.
I tried so hard to make it last

but all too soon it dried away—
I couldn't summon anymore,
and really wondered why I should.

I took an empty bottle
and headed for the berry field
across the way,
not far from home,
leaving at a distance, though,
the wailing,
the gossiping,
one confused ant,
Saturday groceries
and the movies...
A grasshopper and I
decided on a mutual understanding
and settled down
to explore a berry-laden patch
together.

Children always seem to know
the reason
for the cycle!

1986

Coloring Time

I knew that there was something wrong
the day i watched my living room become
an auction block;
and heard the gentle voices
which had always seemed protective,
suddenly with urgency
and ill-concealed pride,
command me to perform and
        earn the admiration
        of our poised and honoured guest
        who, with due consideration,
        and unmitigated awe,
        bought the goods—
        and called my blue eyes,
              honey hair and
              mellow/yellow presence
A WONDERMENT!

WALTER BORDEN

i knew that there was something wrong;
and ran—and hid beneath the steps
'til she had gone;
then took my box of crayons
and filled with calm...and hate,
threw the brown into my dresser drawer,
the white into the fire...
POOR LITTLE SICK BOY.

i knew that there was something wrong
when after i had passed an easy boyhood day
and shared a hundred secrets and
        an apple with my friends,
i was told
i could not go to their house.
it doesn't matter;
you don't need them;
that's what people said—but
yes it did and
yes i did and
any child can tell you
i was right.

still, somehow I walked on, although
i knew that there was something wrong,
and loathed the way that compliments
could flower from contempt
so i became well-schooled
in such gardening,
and weeded out a method
of survival.

i knew that there was something wrong
each time i sat uneasy
in a restaurant
and thought about the laws of equal justice
                that with eloquence
                      and pomp,
                allowed that i could get
              a coke
              but could not rule an
                      attitude,
and there was surely something wrong
when i was asked to overlook such indiscretions,
and then provoked a blazing wrath

FIRE ON THE WATER

when i refused to take the place
you offered me,
and rather chose to seek
              and find my own.

if god is white,
well that's his plight,
not mine;
it would perhaps explain
why there are fringe groups.
if not, then may i say that
yesterday i heard it said
that jesus was a faggot
with twelve lovers
and slept with whores...
sounds like their opinion
of the average black man
who is always thought to start his life
with a spoon[2]
around his neck.

may i humbly recommend
another box of crayons.

Keep It Simple

seems like everywhere i turn these days,
the young folks always tryin' hard
to find out who they is.
mos' of 'em already knows;
they wastin' all that precious time
at tryin' to be what other folkses want.
and that don't make sense to me—
don't make no sense no how, no way!

take Bessie Ann, live down the road;
pretty little thing;
from the day that chile come in this worl';
her mother sayin', all puffed up,
Bessie this and Bessie that
and i got plans for Bessie Ann:
the chile could never say her thoughts.
and 'fore too long her mother tellin' me:
don't want to see my Bessie Ann
with trash that's livin' here;

WALTER BORDEN

soon she git her schoolin' done,
she hittin' out this town.
and you can take that to the bank!
she'll git herself some fine new friends
and be someone important in this town;

she stood right there a year ago,
her hands stuck on her hips,
and said to me:
well thank the lord, i got my wish
and Bessie's on her way;
now mark my words, i see it plain,
Bessie sure will come back big.

and that she did, without a doubt;
eight months big...
and didn't know
what happened to the daddy.

well her mother come a-hootin' and
a-bawlin' and
a-cryin'
and i jes said you git on out my face!
and 'pon my soul, 'fore a week went by,
she beat that chile all black and blue.

one day i'm sittin' on this porch
and hears the racket over yonder;
i says Suzie girl git off this chair,
git down that road
and set them people straight;
and don't you waste no time.

well it must have been a sight, my boy,
for anyone who seen me,
cause my dress was torn,
my head not combed
and my feet was workin' overtime!
and by the time i got down to the house,
i had to sit and catch my bress.
oh, lawd, lawd, lawd, lawd,lawd my boy,
old Suzie was all done in;
but by and by i got some wind
and hollored for to wake the nations:
Lottie Mae—

37

FIRE ON THE WATER

Lottie Mae—
Lottie Mae, girl, where you at?

was nuthin' stirrin', chile,
round that house,
but the crickets and the bees,
so i hobbles up, and looks about,
and drags myself inside.
there's Bessie Ann against a wall,
holdin' on herself,
lookin' like she tryin' to hide a watermelon;
and Lottie Mae's upstairs somewhere
a-sniffin' and a-snortin'.
so up i goes
and there she is;
all laid up
and tryin' hard
to look like she be dead.

oh mama, mama, mama...
i said: don't you dare to mama me,
you overgrown heifer;
and git your ass up off that bed
'fore i slap you round this room!

but mama, mama, all my plans;
i had so many dreams;

yes, i said, i know you did;
but you never dreamed to tell that chile
about a word called no.

remember the simple things, boy.
jes keep it simple!

and Doodle Boy, jes seventeen,
he come to me and say:
i'm gonna be a lady's man—
a cool dude, like daddy.

that right, says i,
well you won't be much
and you won't be one for long.
and don't go blabbin' about your father;
he was walkin' in the devil's shoes

before he left his mama's tit,
and by the time that he was twelve years old,
every girl in this here country
knowed the colour of his drawers.

and that same old fool come in my face
and had the nerve to say:
*my boy will be a real man;
yeah—steady, fast and deadly;*
and true's i'm sittin' in this chair,
a chill went through my bones—

well Doodle Boy roared down that road
and drove hisself to hell;
he wrapped hisself around that tree
and took some young folks with his.
but that what come from heedin' unto others
before you pay a little lissen to yoself!

1986

Mama Don' Tole Me

ain't no use in cryin', chile,
'bout things that you can't change;
jes stand up straight,
clear your eyes
and grab that gravy train
that's goin' somewhere;
there's always one awaitin'
at some station.

an' don't tell that man
that you can't say
your point of destination,
jes speak right up
an' say it clear—
determination pays my fare
an' sweet success will greet me
by an' by…
but don't go lookin' mean.
do your thing
but do it clean.

now after you've achieved your goal
an' things are lookin' fine,

FIRE ON THE WATER

don't go an' blow the whole damn scene
by sayin', what is mine is mine,
an' actin' like you had it all the time.
an' one more thing—
jes because your way was rough,
with some ole thing or other,
ain't no reason why you can't improve it
for your brother.

                                                    1986

Walk On

You must know that you are part of your creator,
And hold within you power to create.
Don't be afraid to fall
At attempting mankind's scale,
Perhaps you're not a singer—
You are a song!
You are a note of ringing splendour
In the universal anthem,
Know your sound—
Know your sound—
You have a life of many pages
To expand the book of ages,
Take a pen, take some ink,
And set it down.
Be a sentence, not a word,
Be of self, and not of herd,
It is your right,
You have the choice
To be your spokesman,
With your voice.

Now step outside your cage
And touch tomorrow.

                                                    1986

The Hebrew Children

...The Hebrew children
Unionized
Under Moses,
Then sat down
On the job

40

WALTER BORDEN

And told old Pharaoh
To fuck himself
And build
His own monuments!

Then God stopped
Gabbing
With the angels
Long enough to promise
Seven plagues for Egypt
If negotiations halted
At the bargaining table

And He delivered!

Ham's descendants
Shouted *HALLELUYAH*,
Caught a train
And travelled
To the Warden of the North[3]
Who counted heads,
Heaved a sigh,
And told them:
Go, and make potatoes
Out of rocks!

Then God stopped
Gabbing
With the Angels
Long enough to promise
Deep investigation into
Segregated schools,
And land titles,
And housing,
And equal opportunity
In general;
And threatened
Every kind of social action.

Last I heard,
God was at
The Lieutenant Governor's
Garden Party
Telling people
It was nice

FIRE ON THE WATER

To see the coloured population
Represented,
And yes, He was preparing
A paper on
Discrimination!

Can I hear an *AMEN*?

1986

Notes
1. A nursery rhyme.
2. Small spoon used for snorting cocaine.
3. Cf. Thomas H. Raddall, *Halifax: Warden of the North*, (Toronto: McClelland and Stewart, 1971).

Frank S. Boyd
1943-

The Politics of the Minority Game: The Decline and Fall of the Black United Front

I. Keep the Faith, Baby: Black Panthers Staying

"I draw the line in the dust," said Alabama governor George Wallace,[1] "and throw the gauntlet before the feet of tyranny, and I say segregation now, segregation tomorrow, segregation forever."

Wallace wasn't the only person throwing down gauntlets in the 1960's. Martin Luthur King[2] told a throng of some 200,000 Americans that he had a dream, "that one day, on the red hills of Georgia, sons of former slaves and sons of former slave-owners will be able to sit together at the table of brotherhood."

Black Nova Scotians were caught up in these strong currents of social change. They responded, in truly Canadian fashion, in a manner that was more orderly, organized and restrained than the black revolution in the United States.

Racism in Nova Scotia was a more discrete business than segregation in Alabama. Colour lines were (and are still) drawn in housing, social services, and community activities, but these lines were quietly enforced. The black community in Nova Scotia had responded to this racist climate by developing its own institutions and by trying to soften the worst aspects of discrimination.

This quiet climate started to change in the 1960's. One key moment was the Nova Scotia Human Rights Federation meeting in Halifax, held on two days beginning Friday, December 6, 1968; and one key element was the perception that the Black Revolution, symbolized by the militant Black Panthers[3], might suddenly come north.

"No Black Panthers will be coming to Halifax to disrupt the human rights conference this weekend," announced black power activist Burnley "Rocky" Jones[4] on Radio CJCH the day before the conference began.

But the presence of the Panthers had stirred the Halifax black community, forcing it to speak out as never before. The Human Rights Federation meeting became a forum for the expression of long suppressed black sentiments.

"The black people in Nova Scotia do not in any way associate themselves with the views of the Black Power movement," said Nova Scotia African Baptist Association moderator the late Ross Kinney.

"We want homes," a black woman from Preston pleaded, "we've got the land... we've got the men; we've got the work power... give us a chance."

"The thing the Panthers have done — which most blacks in Halifax haven't done — is think out the problem... one of the most rewarding ethnic experiences I've had with the Panthers is learning how they think, how they point out the contradictions in the white standard as applied to the black society," said Halifax lawyer Don Oliver.[5]

"Your [white people's] enemy is not Black Power, but ignorance, ignorance of the black man as a human being," said Nova Scotia Home for Coloured Children matron Mary Paris, and she queried: "Can you discern the signs of the times?"

"I see the possibility of violence but if it occurs, it will be an imported thing...spawned by outside agitators," said Baptist minister Rev. Wrenfred Bryant.[6]

"I look to the Black United Front," said Windsor school teacher Wilhemina Williams, "to bring about a new dignity in the Nova Scotia Negro."

At the federation's conference that Friday night, former Progressive Conservative premier, the late Senator G.I. Smith,[7] promised far-reaching changes in human rights legislation. Twenty-four hours later, the Premier announced the appointment of a white, Ontario newsman, Marvin Schiff, to the post of the first full-time human rights director.

Rather than appease black community leaders, the move enraged them. Black leaders claimed that qualified black applicants were ignored. Marvin Schiff, Nova Scotia's first human rights director, had his work cut out for him — his first assignment, to investigate his own appointment.

"I'm bloody mad, and I don't like much what I heard here this morning," Schiff said, "I can only promise you that I'm committed to this job, not just for blacks but for every minority group," adding that "If they [black applicants] got short shift, it makes me very angry."

If there had been any doubt in the minds of black and white people that Black Power was essential to obtaining justice, the hiring of Marvin Schiff changed all that. The Black United Front took hold of the hearts and minds of black as well as many white Nova Scotians. The human rights conference followed by just one week the conception of BUF at a "black family meeting" held in Halifax. At that meeting I was present. We chose to seek black power. Instead we lost our liberty.

II. Seek Black Power, Lose Liberty: The Founding BUF Meeting

In 1969, some black Nova Scotians thought that with $500,000 and the Black United Front they could change the world.

As time has shown, it was not that simple. In their innocence, they did not count on the money and the power changing them, too.

On August 15, 1969, Health Minister John Munro and Minister of State Gerard Pelletier announced a $500,000 grant to BUF. At a press conference in Halifax, Munro described the grant as a means of assisting an under-privileged group to control their own destiny.

On the last day of November, 1968 — a typical frosty-cold and dark November evening — some 400 blacks from around the province met for the first (and only) time, in a black family meeting at the Halifax North End Library.

I, like many others, was seated on the floor of a room full to overcrowding, waiting for what everybody had come to see and hear — the Black Panthers speak.

They spoke eloquently. They were true racemen, stirring everyone's emotions and national pride. They made us determined to change decades of neglect and exploitation — the racist legacy which had so recently destroyed the community of Africville. They gave us pride in being black, a sentiment rarely shared together.

The Black Panthers then stepped aside, yielding the floor to the local leader. When church and statecraft come together as they so often do in the black community, whose power and glory are greater than those of the black preacher?

Rev. W. P. Oliver[8] rose like Moses and eked out the following consensus from the teeming room: to investigate the feasibility of establishing a black united front, similar to the one the Reverend described operating in the United States.

By the time Rev. Oliver spoke to the press several days later, the concept had become a lot clearer to him. A BUF, he explained, would not "take the initiative, in future action, it will be a co-ordinating and catalytic body." It would not be an independent organization, but an "umbrella" for all existing black organizations in the province.

Mandated with this responsibility was an "interim committee." Those appointed that evening: Rev. W.P. Oliver, Burnley "Rocky" Jones, Miss Edith Gray, Ross Kinney, Keith Prevost, H.A.J."Gus" Wedderburn, councillor Arnold Johnson, social worker Buddy Daye and Churchill Smith. In all, these people made up an interim committee of nine.

Assembled in the auditorium that evening was the province's black elite, quite apart from those who just happened to be there by virtue of their proximity to the meeting place. Few realized that in the balance rested job opportunities, new salaries, not to mention career progression — the things which matter most to a highly disadvantaged group[....]

The black family meeting barred all whites, including the press, and denied all white citizens access to a major city-owned institution, a public library auditorium. The glow of Black Power was within us. A segregated meeting, held in a public place, led by a clergyman of the African United Baptist Association, had never occurred before in the long history of blacks in Nova Scotia. Never in our homes, never in our churches or public meeting places, never on festive occasions, but it did happen in a facility owned and operated by the city of Halifax.

It was a perfectly natural reaction to enjoy a meeting from which those whites who had barred us for so long from barber shops and other public places, were now being barred — even though it was only from one isolated, individual meeting. Or so we thought. How they did protest, those who had been barred! And how wrong we were to allow it, and to think of what was happening merely in terms of its publicity, and our personal hidden agendas, rather than in terms of its impact on race relations and on friendships we had enjoyed all our lives!

So the stage was set for a large turnout at the black family meeting. The publicity had worked. I know of no larger turnout of black people to a meeting of this kind in living memory, funerals excepted. However, the price of admission was higher than we thought. Giving away the hard and bitterly earned currency of collective experience in Nova Scotia — the currency of years of indifference, discrimination, joblessness, and the everyday struggle for life — to our "black leaders" of the moment, was a tragic mistake. It was all too easy, all too fast. It seemed to us, then, that time was of the essence.

Perhaps the interim committee's mandate allowed them to select an Ottawa delegation to seek funds to establish a now-feasible BUF, but somehow taking this step seems to have been beyond the power granted the interim committee by the black family meeting. The committee never reported to the black family meeting on the feasibility of BUF. In fact, another black family meeting was *never* held, not even after the committee had acted on its finding that a BUF was feasible. In fact, the committee formed the nucleus for a board of directors who were *never* mandated by the black family meeting.

So it was on these undemocratic foundations that [...]BUF was built. The mechanics of BUF's foundation were ill-conceived, behind closed doors. It is to this legacy of expediency that all past and future BUFs must look for their tradition.

III. Dawn of the Politics of the Minority Game

The Internal Politics

Jules Oliver was hired as executive director when his father had been chairman of the interim committee and then became "special advisor" to and honorary chairman of the board of directors of BUF, but not before his uncle, Halifax lawyer Donald Oliver, resigned as chairman of the personnel committee, charged with the responsibility to recruit, among other personnel, the executive director [...]

Black Nova Scotians were to have the discipline of a political party, but unlike a party, we were to have no control over, or input into, the party's policy-making in any open and public way. If we did not like what we saw in policy, we had no opportunity to vote leaders out of office, or to call a new leadership convention. By the time this had changed — when popular elections were first held on June 8, 1974 — it was more than four years after BUF's official birth.

When the original grant of $500,000 was exhausted and BUF required a fresh mandate, it sought this mandate not at an open and democratic public meeting of the black community, but behind closed doors. Today, in 1984-85, the same "new mandate" has been given, and BUF has a fresh new look — but the same old people are still making the decisions.

At best, it can be said that most of the people involved with the BUF revival still believe in party discipline more than democratic principles. The business of the black community and its organizations are still considered of no concern to anyone else — and those who break the code of silence surrounding BUF are still outcast. It's a grim record the leadership of BUF is holding up for the approval of the black community and the general public.

The code of silence is not just an internal rule of BUF. The silence goes much further, going beyond BUF and making its way into the provincial and federal governments.

The Federal-Provincial Politics

With the new Liberal government in Ottawa and the dying remnants of the Stanfield years on their way out in Nova Scotia, it was easy for black leaders to assume control over their own constituencies through the use of BUF. They aimed to assist in the defeat of the provincial Progressive Conservative government of the day. The provincial Tories put up a good fight for control over the black vote, but BUF had clearly changed the political equation. How black leaders must have relished their new-found power!

The disciplined federal Liberals, always aware of the road to power, had made the ethnic vote a special target. Demonstration grants, such as the $500,000 grant to BUF, served their purpose. That didn't hurt in shoring up the ethnic constituencies, both in Nova Scotia and elsewhere in Canada. They helped achieve the defeat of the Buchanan[9]—and Stanfield-led Progressive Conservatives at home as well as at the national polls.

The Conservatives at home viewed the federal Liberal funding to BUF as an intrusion into their provincial jurisdiction, and for some time refused to co-operate with BUF's leadership. The Conservatives' failure to co-operate held up funding to BUF, but the Tories' inability to win any control over the federal funding left BUF free to kick any sacred provincial cows it chose. The black leaders knew it, and when you got it, you flaunt it.

So long did this animosity endure that BUF's executive director worried out loud whether the provincial funding arrangement that came in under Regan's Liberal provincial government would be honoured when "honest" John Buchanan came to power. BUF's new executive director, Art Criss, had some Conservative credentials — he was a title searcher for the Tory law firm of McInnis, Cooper & Robertson before going to BUF. But still the BUF Council was in worried disarray. The tide in the politics of the minority game had run its course, and now the blacks were caught, like other Liberal organizations, between the Tory 'bleu' and the Liberal 'rouge'.

For some time neither Criss [who, following his conversion to Islam, changed his name to Haamid Rasheed] nor the BUF Council fully understood how a swing in political fortunes could bring about a new growth of political life, allowing a successful transition from Grit to Tory patronage. But those very members of BUF's board of directors who had excelled under Grit patronage, made the transition to Tory patronage without a blush. It was truly a remarkable transition for BUF — other Grit organizations had not been able to flip-flop to Tory patronage quite so easily.

What made BUF different was political opportunism with the highly visible black community. Did the Tories in fact steal a page from the Grit successful string of electoral victories? What price did BUF have to pay to the Tories for a renewed life?

BUF had to change its focus from that of social animation (black consciousness-raising action, i.e., protest) to the delivery of social programs like any other civil service organization. Politically, BUF had to move away from its traditional role of animation to one of inertia, from one of insisting programs be delivered by the provincial government departments to the black community, to one of defending program delivery by both BUF and the provincial government. Provincial government funding muted BUF's voices of protest. The once active organization grew increasingly remote, highly impersonal, and finally irrelevant to the cause of Nova Scotia's black community.

So much for the white-hands-off policy adopted by the black family meeting in 1968. Perhaps BUF could have worked cooperatively with the provincial government. Instead, it allowed itself to be used by the federal Liberals, as it is now being used by the provincial Tories. If black Nova Scotians had had a history of being in the backwaters of Canadian political life until 1968, what a way they chose to come to the fore!

Last Days of Rasheed's BUF

Dubbed a five-year experiment in black self-determination in 1968, BUF was 15 years old when, in 1983, it suffered a funding cut after a government audit revealed "13 areas of concern," which "at worse constitute... a violation of our funding agreement with the BUF and an abuse of public funds."

With the resignation of BUF Council chairman Clyde Bishop, came an announcement of a second audit. The text of Social Services Deputy Minister John A. MacKenzie's seven-page letter, outlining the 13 areas of concern revealed in the first audit, was published in the local press. The entire black community divided on the BUF issue. Liberal Opposition leader Sandy Cameron[10] issued a public statement, accusing the Social Services Minister of ignoring the legitimate concerns of black Nova Scotians. The federal department of the Secretary of State reluctantly froze all future funds to BUF until long overdue activity and financial reports were received. These were some of the more significant events characterizing the last days of Rasheed's BUF.

No stranger to controversy, Rasheed [who retained sole and exclusive control over all financial record-keeping at BUF] dismissed the allegations as a combination of unfair press coverage and "irresponsible" charges from embittered former employees. His worst mistake, however, came at the July 30, 1983, "emergency meeting" of the BUF governing Council, where, in response to accusations [of financial mismanagement], Rasheed countered: "No, no, no! How many more times will I have to say, no!"

[In subsequent "emergency meetings" of the BUF Council that summer, Rasheed admitted to some financial mismanagement.] Still, the BUF Council did not remove Rasheed.

A January 23, 1984 letter from the Social Services Department made clear the provincial government's view of Rasheed's future role within the organization.

"...no provincial funding will be provided...in any event if Mr. Rasheed is to be the chief administrative officer...the department made it clear in its letter of December 23, 1983 that if a proposal [for renewed funding] were submitted showing Mr. Rasheed in any position... he could not have signing authority involving provincial funds."

Rasheed's eventual dismissal was only officially announced by BUF Council chairman Edith Cromwell some two months later, in March, 1984.

Part of the responsibility for the delay lies with Social Services Minister Edmund Morris[11]. The January 23 letter constitutes a complete reversal of his position taken in October, 1983, when Morris issued a statement to the press saying that "They [BUF Council] must take a livelier role in keeping their books in proper form." Regarding demands to freeze provincial funding to BUF the minister said: "We'll not be doing that."

The signal to Rasheed and BUF Council was clear — things were under control, and they relaxed. All the information available to Edmund Morris in January was available to him in October, before he issued his statement clearing BUF on October 20. On October 11, 1983 the Deputy Minister's letter, outlining the 13 areas of concern was received at BUF offices in Dartmouth, so surely the Minister had received his copy of the letter by the time of his October 20 statement. What had happened, then, to change his view?

A shift in public opinion was occurring. By now, the details of the Deputy Minister's letter had been published in the press in their entirety [save appendices], just eight days after the Minister's statement in question. Morris was under *siege* from the black communities' committees — in particular the North Preston Ratepayers — which were agitating for a full public accounting[....]

Perhaps there were other, electoral, reasons for the delaying tactic used by Morris. Perhaps the Tories have learned the lesson the Liberals mastered years before: shoring up the ethnic vote is a basic ingredient for political survival. Morris, MLA for the constituency of Halifax Needham, has more than his share of ethnic voters. His continuing inability to win convincing electoral majorities in Needham seems consistent with his reluctance to cut off BUF funding when all available information suggested that action was the only prudent course.

But if *anyone* was late in taking decisive action, or in getting the message, it was the BUF Council. Even when Rasheed's resignation was announced in March, some Council members wanted him to stay. A BUF insider told the press that "Some of them want to continue without public funding," in order to have Rasheed remain.

Still, the Department of Social Services, in its own words, "continues to be sympathetic to, and available for, funding support of an agency that will effectively and responsibly address the social development needs of black citizens of Nova Scotia." In the Department's eyes, that agency continues to be BUF.

Even before the ballots were cast in the last provincial election, the Minister announced a renewal of funding for BUF. A new BUF staff has been hired and put to work. However — and this is a crucial point — the same board of directors is making the decisions in the same closed-door environment. There has been no talk of a public hearing.

In November, 1968, I glimpsed, along with many other black people, the promise of a truly democratic organization which would unite blacks throughout Nova Scotia in a struggle for social justice.

Instead, the organization born of that movement, BUF, has degenerated into a private, undemocratic, patronage-ridden clique. The democratic impulse has been replaced by bureaucracy and secrecy.

The lack of democracy in BUF has many roots. The long legacy of oppression — from slavery to today's more restrained forms of racism — has provided a poor foundation for democracy. Poverty and dependence produce cynicism and resignation more often than they produce democratic reform movements. But while black Nova Scotians have not really believed in democracy for themselves, the white Nova Scotia elite has not really wanted it for anyone else. Patronage appointments and co-optation have been easier than genuine power-sharing and cooperation. Democracy in Nova Scotia will continue to be thwarted so long as black Nova Scotians hardly believe in it and so long as white Nova Scotians continue to provide ample proof for distrusting it[....]

1985

Notes
1. George Corley Wallace (1919-), governor of Alabama, 1963-1966, 1971-1979, 1983-1987.
2. Rev. Dr. Martin Luther King, Jr. (1929-1968), leader of nonviolent campaign for civil rights for African-Americans. Won Nobel Peace Prize in 1964. Assassinated April 4, 1968.
3. Black Panther Party, U.S. Black political party, founded in 1966, espousing self-defence and socialism.
4. Burnley A. "Rocky" Jones (1941-) is a noted political activist and attorney in Halifax.
5. Hon. Donald C. Oliver (1938-), born in Wolfville, a Halifax lawyer, developer, and Progressive Conservative. Appointed to Senate in 1990.
6. Rev. Wrenfred Bryant (1924-) was born in Verdun, Quebec. Ordained in 1952, he has pastored at many churches in the African United Baptist Association, including Cornwallis Street United Baptist Church (1966-1969). He lives in Lower Sackville.

FIRE ON THE WATER

7. Hon. George Isaac Smith (1909-1982), Progressive Conservative premier of Nova Scotia, 1967-1970; MLA, 1949-1974. Appointed to Senate in 1975.
8. Rev. Dr. William Pearly Oliver (1912-1989), an Africadian religious and political leader. His work appears in this anthology.
9. Hon. John MacLennan Buchanan (1931-), Progressive Conservative premier of Nova Scotia, 1978-1990; MLA, 1967-1990. Appointed to Senate in 1990 amid charges he headed a patronage network.
10. Alexander MacLean "Sandy" Cameron (1938-), businessman, Liberal, Leader of the Opposition in Nova Scotia, 1980-1986; MLA, 1970-1984.
11. Hon. Edmund Morris (1923-), born in Halifax, a journalist; MP, 1957-1963; mayor of Halifax, 1974-1980; MLA, 1980-1988.

Charles R. Saunders
1946-

A Visit to Africville
Summer, 1959

We start at the end of Barrington Street. See where the pavement cuts off and the dirt road begins? That's the "Welcome to Africville" sign. We're still on Barrington Street, you understand. But it's also the old Campbell Road, and it's got a history that goes way, way back in time.

Just call it "The Road." Everybody around here'll know what you're talkin' about.

You can still catch a little whiff of the oil the City sprays to lay the dust. If you look over to your right, you can see the docks of Pier 9. Some of our people work as stevedores down there, and on other docks all over the waterfront. You've got a good view of Bedford Basin from up here. But wait till we get closer to the water. You'll really see something then.

Now we're crossing the first of the railroad tracks that pass through Africville. We call it The High Track, because of the way it slopes upward, like some kind of ski hill. But you ain't seen all the tracks yet. Farther down the road, we got a set of three. They slash through our community like a big pirate's sword. You don't think they had to tear down some houses to put those tracks in? No way to tell which side of these tracks is the right one or the wrong one — you know?

You better believe we learn about trains at a young age here. Trains are a big part of our lives. They can make some noise barrelin' through in the middle of the night! When they had steam locomotives, you used to be able to catch rides on the freight cars. Trains got a rhythm all their own. If you can catch the rhythm, you can catch the train.

We used to get coal that fell off the hoppers and the tender. In the wintertime, you need every piece of coal you can get to heat your house. No more of that, with these growlin' diesel engines. Steam engines sounded friendly; these diesels sound like they want to kill you. And they go too doggone fast.

Can't complain too much about the trains, though. Plenty of our menfolk worked as Pullman porters. Travelled all over Canada and down in the States, they did. Kept those sleepin' cars cleaner than the Sheraton Hotel. They'd come home in their uniforms with the shiny brass buttons, and they'd be like heroes comin' back from a war. Best job a coloured man could get back in the old days. Not so bad now either, if you want to know the truth.

Water, tracks and bushes — that's all you can see right now. Kind of reminds you of the country, even though we're still in Halifax. But you want to see some houses, right? We've walked farther than Jesse Owens ever ran, and you're wonderin' when you're gonna get to see Africville.

Well, take a look up that hill past the tracks. See those houses up there, lookin' like raisins on a layer cake? That's the first part of Africville, if you're comin' in from Barrington Street. We call it Big Town. Don't know why; it ain't even the biggest part of Africville.

You want to know who lives there? The Byers family, the Carters, the Flints, and the Browns. Pay attention to those names, now. You'll be hearin' them again as we go along. Some of our names have a history goin' back to before there ever was an Africville. The first family to settle here was named Brown.

You probably heard of Queenie Byers. She does some bootleggin'. But don't get the idea that everybody here is a bootlegger. It's just another way to get by, that's all. The way some people talk, you'd think Africville was the only place that's got bootleggers.

We do have our fun, though. All kinds of parties. Remember when the soldiers and sailors came back after World War II ended? It was one big party then! If you had a uniform on, you had it made in the shade.

Didn't need a phonograph to get a party goin'. Had plenty of musicians here just as good as what you hear on records. Boysie Dixon could make a piano sing like a bird in the sky. Archie Dixon played the saxophone and clarinet. We had guitar players, fiddlers, and drummers, too. Some folks even made their own instruments. Flutes carved from a tree branch, spoons, washboards—anything and everything! We had people who could sing some, too. You could get a whole concert goin' at the drop of a hat.

Why, we even had some of our people study at the Halifax Conservatory of Music. Ruth Johnson—her name was Brown then—went there. So did Jesse Kane. And Ida Mae Thomas went down to Chicago and ended up playin' the organ for the biggest coloured church in the city.

Now, everybody wants to be Little Richard. That's him on the radio now. They sure don't teach *that* kind of music at the Conservatory. You can have a good time to it, though. Yes, indeed.

Maybe we'll pay a visit up to Big Town on our way back. Bound to be somethin' goin' on. For now, though, let's just keep goin' up The Road.

Look over toward the water. See the big field there? We call that Kildare's Field. It's a good place for picnics. It's also a good place to go swimmin'. Look at those kids divin' off that big rock out in the water. They've probably been there since sunrise. And they'll still be there when the sun goes down.

This field's got some history. Used to be a bone mill there. A lot of our people worked in it, makin' fertilizer. Then the mill shut down, and you can see what's left. Tell you somethin' else. Gypsies come to Kildare's Field every year. They pull up their wagons and stay for about a week or so, tellin' fortunes and all. Some Mamas try to keep their kids away by sayin' Gypsies steal children. But have you ever seen a black Gypsy? Think about it.

Maybe they only steal white folks' kids. Or maybe they don't steal kids at all, and it's just another story like the ones people make up about *us*.

You can see The Road slant downhill now. If you look up toward Big Town, you can't see the houses anymore. Those three tracks are almost like The High Track—up on a slope. This whole area's like a big scoop leading to the Basin.

And now that we're past Kildare's Field, we can see Joe and Retha Skinner's house. It's the first house you get to in Up The Road, or "Africville proper," or whatever you want to call it. You could say this is the "main part" of Africville, if you like to classify things.

Joe's out there bringin' up some water from his well. That's all the water we got here—wells. City says there's too much rock here to put in water lines. Don't make sense—we pay our taxes just like everybody else, but we had to petition the City for telephones and electricity. Ended up gettin' those things. But when we petition for water and sewers, all of a sudden the City goes deaf.

Hi, Joe. How you doin'? No, we're just passin' through right now. Maybe we'll drop by later.

We got to be careful about makin' too many commitments to go to people's houses. When you go to somebody's house in Africville, they're gonna offer you somethin' to eat. And you know better than to turn them down. We got to watch ourselves, or we'll be goin' out of here lookin' like prize pigs.

Speakin' of pigs, people out here used to raise 'em. For a long time there was a slaughterhouse on our outskirts. Once the slaughterhouse shut down, there wasn't no more reason to keep pigs.

Out behind Joe's house you can see Tibby's Pond. It's a tidal pond—you know. When the tide's out, there's a land bridge between the pond and the Basin. When the tide's in, it's all just part of the Basin. It's called Tibby's Pond, because it's on Aunt Tibby Alcock's property.

Whose aunt is she? Well, everybody's. All the older folks here are Aunt or Uncle, Ma or Pa, whether they're related to you by blood or not. It's really like a big family out here. And you know what families are like—lovin' and fightin' all at the same time. Easy to get into; hard to get out of.

Tibby's Pond is where our fishin' boats tie up. All kinds of fishin' goin' on here. Cod, mackerel, halibut, haddock, pollock—we catch all those different fish, just like everybody else in the Maritimes. We get crabs, mussels, and lobsters, too. Imagine poor people eatin' so many lobsters they get sick of 'em! Of course, the fishin' we do is what they call "non-commercial." All that means is, we eat what we catch.

Sometimes you can sell your fish down at the markets on the wharf. But some of the buyers start actin' peculiar when they find out who did the catchin'. God bless 'em.

Next door to Aunt Tibby's is Deacon Ralph Jones' house. His son's house is right beside it. A lot of people build their houses on their parents' property. Keeps the land in the family, deed or no deed.

You can't miss the end of Deacon Jones' lot. That huge tree we're passing is about the biggest property marker you'll ever see. We call it The Caterpillar Tree. That's the only kind of fruit it grows—caterpillars. There's a story behind that tree. A long time ago, Deacon Jones went out and got a post to mark off his land. Next thing he knew, that post was sproutin' leaves, and over the years it grew—and grew. Nobody knows why the caterpillars like it so much.

The Road's startin' to rise again now. See that ocean view? You couldn't buy a better view than that. When the wind's not blowin', the Basin looks like a big sheet of glass. Maybe that's why there's so many houses here. Go ahead, wave to the people; you're among friends.

There's more Browns on this part of the road. There's also Clarence Carvery's place, and Mrs. MacDonald's. Yeah, there's MacDonalds here. What you think, they're all in Cape Breton?

You're noticin' the different colours people paint their houses. Like flowers, right? Folks do what they want to with their houses. If you want to have a different-lookin' door or window, that's OK. Keeps things interestin'.

Down past the Browns' property you can see what we call Back The Field. It slopes down into a gully, then rises back up. That place where those two hills come together is where the kids from Up The Road swim. We play football on Back The Field, too. This is football without helmets or shoulder pads, where you just line up and bust into each other till your Momma calls you in for supper.

We're coming to another driveway now. The house that's closest to the road is Jack Carvery's. He deals in scrap metal from the dump. Yeah, you've heard about the dump. We'll be comin' to it soon enough; don't hold your breath. Those other houses behind Jack's belong to the Carverys, too. Uncle Dook's got a candy store on his first floor. His wife runs it. Then there's Uncle Phum and Aunt Polly's place.

Who knows where those nicknames come from? Childhood, most likely. Sometimes the nickname becomes the real name. Call somebody what it says on their birth certificate, and they'll look at you like you're crazy.

You're beginnin' to notice that Carvery is a pretty common name around here. So is Brown, Mantley, Howe, and Dixon. You got to be careful who you get involved with—it might be your cousin. Older folks know every root and branch of the family tree, though. They'll keep you out of trouble.

Here's Aunt Hattie Carvery's place. She runs our Post Office. Address a letter to Africville, Nova Scotia, and it'll get here, all right. No, Aunt Hattie. Don't want to see no mail today. Probably nothin' but bills.

Let's go down this other driveway. Bertha Mantley's house is right on The Road. Behind it, there's a small house that gets rented out to different people. And then there's Bully Carvery's place. Don't have to tell you how he got that name. He's a hard rock. You don't want to mess with him.

You say you want to keep goin'? OK, we'll head back to The Road. Didn't mean to make you nervous. There's Curley Vemb's house. That's his real name, all right. He's a Norwegian. Married an Africville girl and moved out here. Gets along just fine.

Now you're lookin' at a whole string of houses. They all got front yards to separate 'em. Sarah Byers and Edward Dixon live here. And there's Pooh Izzard's place. Pooh's a prizefighter. Trains up at the Creighton Street Gym. How you doin', Pooh? Good luck in your next fight.

Now we're passin' the homes of Bill Gannon, John Tolliver, and Bub Cassidy. And if you look over to the other side of the road, just where it starts to bend, you'll see the church. Seaview African United Baptist Church, to be exact.

Let's go over to the church and stop for a minute. Look at the way that white paint gleams in the sun. Look at the steeple standin' against the sky. Now, be perfectly quiet. Tune out the sounds of the kids and the cars and the dogs.

Listen close...can you hear it? Can you hear that sound, coming from the church? It's like a heartbeat...the heartbeat of Africville. This church is the living, breathing soul of our community. Long as this church is here, *we'll* be here.

We pretty well have to run the church ourselves. Ain't enough money here to pay a full-time minister. We get visitin' preachers from places like the Cornwallis Street Church in the City and Saint Thomas Church in North Preston. Old Reverend Wyse[2] used to walk all the way from Lake Loon to preach to us. We've had some of the best in our pulpit—Reverend White[3], Reverend Skeir[4], Reverend Oliver[5], and Reverend Coleman[6].

Now we got Reverend Byrant[7]. On Sundays when he can't come out here, the deacons take over. And some of those deacons can really rock your soul once they get goin'.

And the singin'! You'd have to go a long, long way before you could find singin' like you get here. It's like the people put all their soul in their voices, then send it straight on up to God's ears.

But you know it takes more than singin' and preachin' to make a church. Church got to be more than just a place you get dressed up to go to every Sunday. Especially in a place like Africville, where we don't have our own mayor or city council or policemen. Church got to be all those things wrapped up in one. All kinds of business goes on in this church, and not just on Sunday. We got clubs, youth organizations, ladies' auxiliary, and Bible classes. You want to get somethin' done here, you get it done through the church.

Funny thing—not everybody 'round here goes to church on a regular basis. We got our share of sinners and backsliders: folks who only set foot there on Christmas and Easter, and others who don't set foot here at all and don't mind tellin' you so. But you know what? Even those folks say this is "our" church. It belongs to everybody, whether they go or not.

You ought to come out here next Easter for Sunrise Service. That's the biggest day of the year in Africville. Folks from all over Nova Scotia come here to take part. Got to warn you, though. Be prepared to get up early. Service begins at five in the morning, soon as the sunlight starts to fillin' the Basin.

Yes indeed, folks take that day seriously. Most people spend the whole night gettin' their clothes ready and their kids washed. When you're young, you don't even sleep that night. You're wide awake when your Momma comes in to get you up while it's still dark outside.

By the time the preacher's ready to start his sermon, the church is full. You could be listenin' to Reverend Byrant or maybe somebody from farther away. We sing those old-time spirituals to the tune of organ and piano music. If you want to hold hands and sway to the music, that's OK. If you want to stand up and testify, nobody's stoppin' you. Everybody's got their own way to get close to the Lord and each other.

The worship goes on till about noon. Then it's time for the baptism. We do baptisms all year long, but there's something special about bein' baptized on Easter.

You can see the candidates dressed in their white baptismal robes. They might look a little nervous on the outside, but inside, they're strong. They'll line up behind the Reverend, and the rest of the congregation lines up behind them. Then the Reverend leads us all from the church down to the Basin. It's a long procession. Each step you take, you realize that your grandparents took it before you, and their grandparents took it before them.

Then we reach the shoreline. Men, women, and children, all lookin' wide-eyed with wonder at the beauty of the Basin. The singin' goes on; it doesn't stop even when the Reverend begins the baptisms. Don't need a choir. The whole congregation is the choir. Our voices lift up while the candidates get immersed in cold sea water. Salt water—just like the first baptism that was performed in the Sea of Galilee.

Then we go back to the church. The candidates are wet and happy. Everybody else is happy, too. Some of the people go back to church; others go home to celebrate in their own way. The young ones get to eat all the eggs they want. That's probably what they been thinkin' about all day, anyhow.

Still, some of the meaning of Sunrise Service rubs off on them. One day, they'll be the ones to go into the water. And they'll know this is a day when Africville shines.

Didn't mean to go on like that. But if you want to understand Africville, you got to know about the church. Then again, you heard the heartbeat. So you do understand. Let's keep goin'. There's more of Africville to see.

Right next to the church is the old school. They closed it down back in '52. We use it for recreation now. See the swings, still standin' in the playground?

It sure was a sad day when that school shut down, and our kids had to walk all the way up to Richmond School from primary on. When children come up from Africville, it's like there's a sign on their forehead saying "Auxiliary Class." You know what that is, don't you? That's where they put the "slow learners."

First thing you got to do at Richmond is prove you're not a "slow learner." Why? Well, once they get you in that Auxiliary Class, you can't get out. It's like bein' caught in a lobster trap. You might as well say your education's over right then and there.

Wasn't like that when we had our own school. Went all the way up to Grade Eight, it did. Only had one room, but that room was partitioned in two sections. One was for the lower grades; the other for the "big kids." Times bein' what they were, it was hard to stay in school. So many of us had to quit in order to help support our families. But if you could stick it out in that school, you got an education. You could go on to Queen Elizabeth High or Saint Pat's, and know you could hold your own with the other kids.

There were some good teachers at that school. Everybody down here remembers old Mr. Jemmott. Could be even his wife didn't know his first name; he was just "Mister Jemmott." He was from the West

FIRE ON THE WATER

Indies. That man taught for twenty-five straight years without missin' a single day. His son, Gordon, ended up bein' the principal, and Gordon was just as strict as his old man.

Those black teachers did us proud. John Brown was the first one. Then there were other Jemmotts: Clyde and Clarice. Teachin' sure ran in that family. People remember Laylia Grant and Verna Davis, too. And Portia White[8] taught in our school for a while. Can't that woman sing! But she could teach, too. No doubt about that.

Well, the school's gone now. Can't do nothin' about it. Let's keep goin'.

There's our old friends the triple tracks. Remember how they were risin' up? Well, now they're level with us again. We're gonna stop at this bend here. Take a look all around you. Right here is where you can see all of Africville—the whole layout.

Look back where we came from, and you can see Big Town and Up The Road. Now take a look in the other direction. See those houses peekin' out from behind those woods? That's Round The Bend, the third part of Africville. We'll be goin' there shortly. But there's still more to see right here.

We're gonna be delayed anyhow. Here comes a train. Lord, that noise is terrible! Sounds like an avalanche thunderin' right past you.

There's Dick Killum's house. Look past it, and you'll see a level field. We call it The Southwestern. It's a sports field, mostly. There's some buddies out there now playin' softball. We play horseshoes there, too. In the wintertime, the whole thing freezes over, and you can play hockey on it. You ever hear of the Africville Brown Bombers? The team Gordon Jemmott coached? That's where they practiced.

Back in the old days, the Basin used to freeze over, and they played hockey out there. Imagine playin' hockey on part of the Atlantic Ocean! Can't do that nowadays. Winters ain't what they used to be. Nothin' is.

Fellas here play hockey just for the fun of it. Ain't lookin' to get in the NHL. NHL ain't ready for no Jackie Robinson[9] yet, so they say. Every now and then, though, somebody gets ideas. Once there was this boy who wanted to be a goalie. He'd be out there on the Southwestern every day, stoppin' rubber balls and whatever else kids used instead of pucks.

Well, one day his cousins get hold of a real puck. They start shootin' it around, practicin' that newfangled rifle shot. Buddy figures he was gonna stop that puck just like he stopped all those rubber balls. So he sticks his leg out, with nothin' on it but his pants.

KA-RACKKK!

You could hear the sound all the way over in Big Town. And that's one boy who didn't play no more goal that day.

Train's gone at last. Let's cross the field and go behind that little hill. There's more houses back that way. We're still Up The Road, understand. This is just a different neighborhood.

Hold it. Got to throw this ball back. Catch it next time, Cousin! Yeah, right! In your dreams!

Those boys wouldn't be so smart if they remembered how good the girls' teams were back in the 40s. The Africville Ladies' Softball Club, that's what they called it. White blouses, black skirts, and a winnin' attitude. Gordon Jemmott coached them. They used to play all over the Province—Stellarton, New Glasgow, places like that. One year, they took the Provincial championship.

The three Brown girls were on that team—Lucinda, Jessie, and Ruth. There was Wilhemina and Alma Dixon, Amy Carvery, Stella Dixon, and Evelyn Jemmott, too. Those ladies are all married and settled down now. But you know what? They could still come down here and send those boys runnin' to their Mommas.

There's Aunt Tillie Newman's house. Her daughter Ivory Marsman lives right next door. You can see more houses in a line going toward the water. First there's the old Gannon place. Minky Carvery lives there now. Pauline Dixon and Dora Dixon have the next two houses.

See that shed? That's Uncle John's card room. The men go there when they want to play some serious cards. You don't get cut an inch of slack in *that* shed!

Now we're at a bigger hill. We call this one Uncle Laffy's Hill. That's where kids ride their sleds in the winter.

Best time to go down that hill is late at night when the moon's out. Seems like it takes forever before your Momma and Poppa go to sleep. Half the fun is sneakin' out the door with your sled, or piece of cardboard, or whatever you want to use.

When the moon's full or close to it, you might as well be in daylight. It's like the world's turned into one big black-and-white snapshot. And the kids are part of the picture.

We get up to the top of the hill...then WHOOOSH! Down we go! When the snow's got a crust of ice on top of it, you zoom down so fast Africville turns into a speeded-up movie, everything flashin' past before you can get a good look at it. And you don't make any noise, either. You go zippin' through the trees and between the houses like some kind of ghost.

Well, it sure ain't wintertime now. Tell you who lives up on Uncle Laffy's Hill these days. Whoppie Sparks lives there. He runs a penny store. There's Dixons, Howes, and Carverys there, too. And you'll also find Leon and Emma Steed in that neighborhood. Leon came from the West Indies; Emma is a Carvery.

FIRE ON THE WATER

We could climb up to the top of the hill, but you want to see Round The Bend before it gets dark. So we'll take a different way. We can just skirt around to the other side of the hill and head back to The Southwestern.

You can see the Paris house at the bottom of the hill. Now, look way up. There's the High Track. Remember we crossed it when we first came down Barrington Street? More folks live along the road that follows the track. Another Paris family's up there, and there's more Dixons.

You say you're gettin' thirsty? Let's head to Whoppie's store and get some pop before we go on.

How you doin', Whoppie? Can we get two Cokes? Thanks. Naw, can't stay too long. We're takin' the Grand Tour of Africville. More to it than there seems to be, right? That's what people always say when they come here for the first time. See you later, Whoppie.

Want to show you a couple more houses past The Southwestern before we go Round The Bend. You see the horseshoe curve over there? Roy Mantley lives down that way. So does Lee Carvery. What's that? You say there's more Carverys around here than there are trees? Don't get smart. We can always go back to Uncle Bully's, you know.

Now we're following the curve of the triple tracks. Your nose is wrinklin' already, like it wants to be someplace else. That's a sure sign we're gettin' close to the dump, over on the water side. Doggone thing's only been here a few years, and already people associate it with us. Or us with it. They take our school away and give us a friggin' garbage dump!

Well, when bad times hit you, you can just lay down and die. Or you can keep on goin' and make the best of it. So we try to make the dump work for us. Just because somebody throws something away, that don't mean you can't use it.

Looks like a mountain of trash and junk, doesn't it? But it's not all bad. There's all kinds of scrap metal in there that you can collect and sell. Copper, steel, brass, tin—all of it's worth somethin'. You got to know what you're doin', you understand. There's ways of tellin' good stuff from bad stuff. You got to learn, just like any other trade. They call it "salvaging."

Car parts. That's another one. We got fellas here who can get parts off the dump and make the worst-lookin' wreck in the world run like new. One time, a couple of buddies put together a whole car from scratch and drove it to Winnipeg! Did they drive it back? Naw. If it didn't fall apart, they probably sold it. Somebody out there now could be drivin' an "Africmobile."

You know what really gets up folks' behinds out here? When those newspapers talk about us "scavenging" food and clothes off the dump.

People read that stuff and think we're runnin' around diggin' week-old tomatoes and nasty rags out of that messy dump. Any fool knows you get stuff off the trucks *before* they throw it on the dump. Doesn't hurt the drivers to give us day-old bread or leftover meat every now and then. They do the same thing for people who live near other dumps.

We get clothes from them, too. By the time the ladies out here get through workin' with their needle and thread on second-hand clothes, you'd never know they were bound for the dump.

Some folks say the dump was put here to try to drive us out. If that's true, things kind of backfired, didn't they?

Well, we could stand here talkin' about this place all day. But it ain't the most pleasant way to spend an afternoon, so let's go Round The Bend.

First houses you see here are are Mrs. Thomas' and Dan Dixon's, right off the tracks there. That other house belongs to Lucy Carvery. Up toward the High Track is Deacon George Mantley's place, and right next to it's Willie Carvery's. And then there's Pa Carvery's house. "Uncle Pa," everybody calls him. If he's not your grandfather or great-uncle, he ought to be. Pa's got a little store, too. It's in the other part of Round The Bend, past these woods.

That's right. We got our own little forest here. Used to be a lot more woods and bush around, but most of it got cut down for lumber and firewood. Nothin' but young trees and alder bushes and wildflowers now. We'll just follow this little path here, and we'll be all right.

See that pond over there? We call it our "lake," even though it ain't really all that big. When the sun hits it right, it looks just like a jewel.

No need to be scared of that dog. Any dog that shouldn't be loose, we keep chained in a shed. Don't tell that to the cops, though. Some of 'em come up here with their huntin' jackets on and shoot our dogs like they was in season.

Go on home, boy. That's right. Got nothin' for you here.

Well, that's the end of the woods. We're in the last part of Africville. Some of those houses we're lookin' at now got runnin' water and indoor toilets. They're far away from all that "unbreakable" rock the City keeps tellin' us about when we want to get water lines put in.

There's Lully Byers' house. Yeah, that's Lully hangin' her wash on the line. Her real name's Wilhemina. But don't ever call her that, or she;ll hang *you* out to dry.

There's Rossie Dixon's place. And the Emersons'. Reggie and Stella Carvery are here, and Ronald and Sooks Howe. Pa Carvery's store's out here, too.

Did you know Joe Louis[10] stayed at Rossie's house one night? Yeah, Joe Louis. The Brown Bomber himself. We used to listen to his fights all the time on Jamesie Paris' radio. He had one of those old RCA radios with the big horn.

You remember when Joe came to Halifax a few years ago to referee some rasslin' matches? That's how he had to make his livin' when he gave up the heavyweight title and then couldn't get it back.

Anyhow, the promoter for the rasslin' put him up in one of those downtown hotels that usually don't take coloured guests. Well, when Joe got wind of that, he checked right out of that hotel. You know how Joe was. Never would put up with no discrimination.

Then ol' Joe went lookin' for the coloured folks part of town, and he ended up here. When he found out he'd be stayin' with a Dixon, he just lit right up with a smile. Turns out he knew all about George Dixon[11], the first coloured man to win any kind of prizefightin' championship. Well, you know George was born in Africville, and every Dixon here is some kind of a relation of his. So Joe felt right at home, stayin' with a Dixon.

Seemed like half of Halifax was out here lookin' to shake Joe's hand or get his autograph. That was some night for Africville, let me tell you. When Joe left the next day, he looked like he was sorry he had to go.

But you know, Joe Louis wasn't the only famous person to come to Africville. Remember Reggie and Stella Carvery's place? Well, Duke Ellington[12] stops by there all the time. That's right, the one and only Duke.

There's a story behind that, too.

Duke's wife's name is Mildred Dixon. She was born in Boston, but her father was an Africville Dixon, and he never forgot where he came from. Stella Carvery's a Dixon, too—Mildred's her cousin.

Mildred was a ballet dancer. Duke took one look at her and BOOM—he was in love. They got married down in New York.

Now Mildred was Duke's second wife. He had a son named Mercer by his first one. Mildred was the one who raised Mercer; far as he was concerned, she was his Mama. And every time Duke brings his band to Halifax, he comes out here to see his in-laws. Mercer comes this way, too. And Duke gives us free tickets to his concerts.

Remember that song of his, "Sophisticated Lady"? That's about Mildred. Next time you listen to the Duke's music, maybe you'll remember there's a little bit of Africville in it.

You know, that's one of the reasons why we don't pay much mind when people talk down to us. If we're good enough for folks like Joe Louis and Duke Ellington, we figure we're darn well good enough for anybody else.

Well, we're just about at the end of our trip. The Highways Board Building and the Fairview Overpass—that's the end of Africville.

CHARLES R. SAUNDERS

Sure, you're welcome to stick around. Stop by for supper, we'll be glad to have you. Stay overnight, too, if you want. Always room for one more here.

And when you get back home, if anybody asks you about Africville, you just tell 'em we been through good times and hard times, but we're still here. Yeah, there's been talk about gettin' us out of here.

"Relocation," they call it. But we've heard that kind of talk before. Long as it's just talk, we got nothin' to worry about, right?

1989

Notes

1. Africville, originally called Campbell Road Settlement, was a Black village which nestled on the shores of Bedford Basin in north end Halifax. Founded in 1815, it was bulldozed by the City of Halifax in the late 1960s and its residents relocated.
2. Rev. Arthur A. Wyse (1867-1953) received only 2 1/2 days of schooling. Began preaching at age 26; ordained at age 48.
3. Rev. Dr. William Andrew White (1871-1936), of Truro, was the only Black chaplain in the British Army in World War I. He was also the first African-Canadian to gain a doctorate (Divinity, Acadia University, 1936).
4. Rev. Donald D. Skeir (1927-), born in Halifax, has served as pastor to the Prestons and Cherrybrook since 1953.
5. Rev. Dr. William Pearly Oliver (1912-1989) led Africadians in the fields of religion, education, and human rights. His work appears in this anthology.
6. Rev. Charles L. Coleman, U.S.-born, led protests in Harlem, New York, before moving to N.S., where he was a pastor, 1962-1965. He returned to the U.S., where he still lives.
7. Rev. Wrenfred Bryant (1924-) was born in Verdun, Quebec. He was ordained in 1952 and pastored at Africville's Seaview United Baptist Church from May 1966 to October 1967. He lives in Lower Sackville.
8. Portia White (1911-1968), of Truro, was a contralto and music teacher. Debuted at New York's Town Hall in 1944; gave Command Performance before Queen Elizabeth II in 1964. Famed for her *bel canto* technique, she sang in English, French, German, and Spanish, and recited both spirituals and classical songs.
9. John Roosevelt "Jackie" Robinson (1919-1972) was first Black baseball player to join a major league team during the xx century. Elected to Hall of Fame in 1962.
10. Joe Louis Barrow (1914-1981), a U.S. boxer, was world heavyweight champion, 1937-1949. Called the "Brown Bomber" for his quick, devastating punches.
11. George Dixon (1870-1909), of Africville, a boxer, became the World Bantamweight Champion (1890) and the World Featherweight Champion (1891). Dubbed "Kid Chocolate," he died of alcoholism and opium addiction.
12. Edward Kennedy "Duke" Ellington (1899-1974) was a U.S. jazz musician and composer. After meeting dancer Mildred Dixon at the Cotton Club in Harlem, New York, in 1929, Ellington left his wife, Edna. Though Dixon and Ellington lived common-law for ten years, they never married. "Sophisticated Lady" was composed in 1932; hence, it might have been written with Dixon in mind. See James Lincoln Collier, *Duke Ellington* (Oxford: Oxford University Press, 1987), pp. 102-103.

Gloria Wesley-Desmond
1948-

Back Alley Tramp

Walk some dark and
Smothering night until you
Somehow find yourself
Alone, haunting the bleakness
Of the alley. Alone, except
For a few restless, hungry
Creatures rubbing their
Dirty backs against some
Over-turned can; and
Slinky rats speed along
The base of towering brick
Buildings—cold, sooty, rigid.

Walk down the narrow
Way of poisoned minds,
No church bell chimes
A beckoning plea to come.
I stoop to betray some
Emotion, a subconscious
Pang for someone upon whom
I can lean for an instant.
Back doors stare into
My face as if they dare
To shoot me down to back-door welcomes.
They smirk at me, as I walk past,
With their grimy panes,
And cracked wood veins.
They hang limp off
Broken, rusty hinges.
How dare they laugh at me?

The silence of the night
Has been disturbed by
The meows of shabby cats
Following close behind my heels.
I keep searching, tearing
At my brain, ripping at my

GLORIA WESLEY-DESMOND

Hollow soul to find no trace
Of feelings, no origins for
Concrete thoughts.
The coldness of night
Nips at my scrawny body
And hugs my heart as
Though it were a kindred
Spirit from the Frigid Zone.

And I walk, onward
Toward a glistening street
Lamp peeking through the
Daze of sleepy night!
Onward into a night
That abounds with fears
And window pane stares
Of people locked inside
Themselves.
How dare they stare at me?

They, with their artificial
Roses, Salvation Army boxes,
Watered-down beer and
Back alley tears!
Don't stare at me!
Don't stare at me!
You gave me these boundaries—
Of alley dirt and fears,
I'm your product,
I'm your child,
Your back alley tramp!

1975

The Sea at Night

High above head,
The loud screeches
Of silver-winged
Gulls—circling,
Circling, circling,
Below the huge
Rocks, the sound of
The surf, crashing,
Rumbling, pounding
Violently upon the

FIRE ON THE WATER

Slimy rocks—slippery,
Hanging with gelid[1]
String of dark
Brown seaweed.
How deep the night!
Listen to the splash
Of the waves, white-
Capped, frothing,
Cold, scary, impenetrable!
Waves, thundering,
Thundering! Crashing
To their death.
How deep the night!
Listen—the lonely fog
Horn blows feebly into
The night, warning little
Boats, trawlers, and the
C.N.[2] Ferry of their fate,
Their impending death,
Among the rocks,
Mist, wet, cold
Mist that soon
Will smother the
Coast.
Blurring my vision,
Chilling my soul,
How deep the night!

1975

To Nova Scotian Blacks

Children of darkness,
Torn and battered,
You have slipped the savage
Bonds of slavery.

Children of darkness,
Full of courage,
Strength and endurance,
You have survived.

Children of darkness,
Facilitating equality,
Rise up and take
The reins of your destiny!

1992

GLORIA WESLEY-DESMOND

Defeat

To admit defeat
   Means never having
   The right to eat in a restaurant,
   The right to sit downstairs at a theatre,
   The right to fight for one's country,
   The right to be a store clerk, nurse, or secretary,
   The right to cross color-lines in marriage,
   The right to live on the east-side,
   The right to learn about yourself.
To admit defeat
   Means never having
   Been freed at all.

                                                1992

Jump the Broom

Mama, mama,
Where can he be?
We jump the broom[3]
At half past three.
My master, he says,
It be all right
To dance and party
All the night.
The fiddle is tuned,
The food is hot,
Chicken and dumplin
In every pot.
Aunt Nisha, she says,
I sure be in gold
And I must pray
We never be sold.

Oh, mama, the time,
It's drawin near,
And my ol' man
He should be here.
But somethin be wrong,
I feel a chill,
The dogs be barkin
Down by the mill.
Come quick, mama!
Come quick as you can!

FIRE ON THE WATER

Them dogs be chasin
My ol' man.
See him runnin
Through the trees;
That be him;
God, help him please!

What's that I hear?
A shot? Can't be!
My man, he's fallin
On his knees.
His weddin shirt
Be soaked with blood,
His feet be draggin
In the mud.
His master be comin
With a rope and gun;
My ol' man
Can't get up to run.
Mama, mama,
This just can't be,
We jump the broom
At half past three!

1992

Braids

"Ouch!
Mama that hurts!
Why you got to be
Pullin and tuggin
With that ol' hard brush?
I hate braids!"
And all the while
Mama be sayin—
"Girl, you got some wool!"
an'
"Hold that head still, girl!"
an'
"What I gonna do with this stuff?"
Then,
Finally—
Jus one last stroke,
Those fingers be windin, pullin,
and twistin with lightning speed

70

and—
There I am,
Standin with big red ribbons
Tied up in fancy bows,
struttin out to first grade
And thinkin—
My kids are gonna go
AFRO![4]

1992

Let's Parta
There ain't nothin like
    Saturday night
When the brothers "be"
    In sleek, satin threads,
    Holdin heads high and
    Struttin their stuff.
When sisters step out
    Tossin curled heads and
    Sassy—Lawd—Sassy
And soul food,
    The aroma embracing,
    Tantalizing your nostrils.
And music.
    Loud, pulsating music
    Forcing you to move and groove,
    And slick out-of-town dudes
    Pullin you in tight-mm-tight!
Everybody be
    Grinnin, jivin, shoutin,
    Teasin and gettin down.
Ain't nothin like
Partaing with
    The brothers and sisters!

1992

Outrageous

Damn you men of my race,
You are fools to think
Black women want to play
Second fiddle to your
white
desires!

1992

FIRE ON THE WATER

Black Men

How I adore you black men,
With your smooth,
slippery
skins,
Your big, bold grins,
And tremendous arms to rest in.
Such grinning, evil eyes,
You are musky,
sensuous,
stimulating.
You are beautiful
and I love you.

1992

Notes
1. Icy.
2. Canadian National Railway, a corporation which once operated the East coast, inter-provincial ferries.
3. A slave marriage ceremony ritual.
4. A hairstyle natural to African peoples; it was popular from 1967 to 1978.

Maxine Tynes
1949-

I am Maxine Tynes. I am a woman. I am Black. I am a poet. Four basic truths. None chosen. All joyful in my life.

As a writer, I know that this creative process was not 'chosen' by me, consciously, as part of my life. The pursuit of The Muse; the passion of holding life and love and thought and feeling, and of handling them through words is not a consciously engineered selective process. It is not selected from a list of choices of being, perhaps, a clerk, a stone mason, a nurse or doctor, or a weaver.

It is, rather, an urge as strong, natural and uncontrollable as an urge to laugh, to weep, to sleep, to hold one's beloved.

To write is powerful medicine, magic, weaponry and love.

To write poetry is the ultimate in that power. It is a sweet and yielding power, as well as being an incisive and bludgeoning one.

Terrorist and oppressive regimes know this only too well. In Chile,[1] Nicaragua,[2] Northern Ireland,[3] in Johannesburg,[4] under Naziism or Fascism, the poets, the singers, the writers, the storytellers are among the first to be muzzled, silenced and to disappear.

I write from a deep, eternal and eclectic energy of my own making and that of all of those who have touched my life in my own time, as well as in the distant past before my own lifetime.

When I write, I feel the hand of my mother, Ada Maxwell Tynes; of my sisters; of my grandmothers on both and on all sides; of my father Joseph James Tynes; of my brothers; and of all the men and women in my life.

When I write, I feel the depth of my Blackness, and the spread of my Blackness through, and by, and beyond the poems and the stories of Black culture, Black life and Black womanhood that I put on paper.

My Blackness is as real to me in my poems as it is to me as I see my own Black hand move my pen and these words across the page.

My Blackness, my culture and Black ethnicity becomes a shared thing then with those who are and are not Black like I am. I love that. To see the recognition of Black personhood in the eyes of others who share my history. To see the wonder, that curious mix of fear and wonder becoming awareness of same and different and the o.k. ness of it all in those Caucasian or other eyes. I love that.

All of that from writing. All of that as a wonderful ethereal return for being a poet. That rare and wonderful state of being which I did not choose; yet, joyfully, I am.

I am Maxine Tynes. I am a woman. I am Black. I am a poet.

1986

FIRE ON THE WATER

The Profile of Africa

We wear our skin like a fine fabric
we people of colour
brown black tan coffee coffee cream ebony
beautiful, strong, exotic in profile
flowering lips
silhouette obsidian planes, curves, structure
like a many-shaded mosaic
we wear our skin like a flag
we share our colour like a blanket
we cast our skin like a shadow
we wear our skin like a map
chart my beginning by my colour
chart my beginning by my profile
read the map of my heritage in
my face
my skin
the dark flash of eye
the profile of Africa.

1980

Black Song Nova Scotia

We are Africville and Preston,
North and East
We are Portia White[5] singing to a long-ago king
We are Edith Clayton[6] weaving the basketsong of life
Black and old with history
and strong with the new imperative.
We are Graham Jarvis[7] bleeding on the road in Weymouth Falls.
We are the Black and the invisible
We are here and not here
We are gone but never leave
We have voice and heart and wisdom
We are here
We are here
We are here.

1990

Chameleon Silence

I feel very Indian tonight
very Micmac[8]
      Kuakiutl[9]
      Huron[10]
and Black
my tongue growing back 200, 500 years.
I speak in beauty
the truth of earth and sky
virgin breath of
who I am
what I feel.

you don't hear the roots and leaves
of my words
hanging like black veins from my lips
you clip the hedge
and build a railway through the field and rock
and stream of my words
like your three-times gone granddaddy did
under the maple sky.

tonight this Black woman sleeps on
the blood-carpet of broken treaty-dreams of long ago.

But this is 1985.
And tonight I know,
like a maidenhead just gone
why, Indian woman,
you are me.

                                              1987

4. When the Setting is my Classroom
(from "The Portrait Poems")

then I am all of my Blackest self
artist, darken your palette
black the to and fro of me
make black punctuation
of all of my dimensions
the crook of my arm, a sleek
black comma
we will go on and on and on
my eyes, the end point of exclamation

FIRE ON THE WATER

I black the air with the rush of
words from my lips
artist, artist, make ebony your brush
canvas black me to the world.

                                                                  1990

Silent Crows

And now your feathered night-blackness is gone
freeing branches to the light and
to the weightlessness of day.
Without you,
without your black punctuation
the sky, the trees have no endpoint.
My eyes dart and dart
and, finding no crow-blackness,
wait for the night.

                                                                  1990

Bury My Heart by Degrees

Don't fall out of love in a small town like Halifax
restaurants
and rounding street corners
are deathtraps and
uncertain rendez-vous for old lovers;
one strong and flaunting heartlessness
and a new lover;
one is a shadow
and fragile
and trying to slip the skin of memory
but it fits too tight
parts cling
and grow back
and do not yield to picking at old wounds.

                                                                   1990

MAXINE TYNES

The Call to Tea
To commemorate Portia White, classically trained operatic singer of great international reputation during the 1940s. A great Black Maritime woman.

The call to tea
a solid knell of the social register
in old Halifax
silk moire[11]
dank velvet
crepe and lace splayed across settee
mahogany and divan
the shadow of servers
invisible in stiff black stuff
laying table
just so, with the delicacy of
cucumber, tea-cake and scone
on porcelain and silver
filigree of lacy oak leaf shadow
through a southend Halifax window.

To be so owned and distanced
to be called to tea
to have opened that dark and silver throat
and poured sweet amber liquid
upon the crowned heads of England
and of Europe and left them wanting;
to have New York and great Carnegie
glittering and applauding behind and
around and ever after that dusky
dusky throat.

To be so owned and distanced
to be called to tea
Miss W____,
so dusky proud and unassuming
to own and execute that throat of miracles
to sit, owned and distanced,
this daughter of old Halifax
this feted lady of the world stage
to feel the shudder of upscale lashes seeking presence
denying connection
translucent skin retracting
peeling back vacant smiles
the hollow ring of truth not spoken
this parody of social tea

FIRE ON THE WATER

oak shadows filigreed and fallen
through prestigious southend window

The tea, finding path down and
down that dusky throat
the elixir of that moment
poured so elegantly by some pale and glittering I.O.D.E.[12] arm.

To be so owned and distanced
to be called to tea in genteel Halifax
of that era
so fresh from singing to some king,
some prince or president.

Later, one of them would say,
"It was so hard not to ask her to go down to the cellar
to fetch a scuttle of coal."

1990

For Tea and not for Service

The ticking of the clock was like a heartbeat in that oh so correct and perfect room. That Southend parlour, so well appointed with its fullness of oak and plush velvet and its surround of windows heavy with lace.

There she sat. Small and dark and such a counter-point to everything around her today in this room, in this house, with these people. These pale women.

The Imperial Daughters had asked Celie to tea. And so she had come to tea. After the surprise of the invitation and the rounds and rounds of talk at home about that invitation, Celie had come to the Imperial Daughters' tea. A small smile as she replayed the at-home talk about the invitation. Even the white vellum card had been weighed, passed from one worn, dark hand to another. She had assured her folks that, yes, indeed, that ragged creamy edge was as it should be, a sign of value and quality and not discard paper. Even the handwriting, black and elaborate like bits of some insect's wings, had been scrutinized and remarked over.

"Hmph! Would you look at that! Couldn't even send your invite on decent paper. Looks torn out of somethin' to me."

That was Celie's mother. And some variation of the same was offered by the aunts and the others until Celie assured them that, no, this was indeed some good, heavy white vellum notepaper, complete with watermark — showing them how to look for it — and probably from the Boston States.[13]

Celie smiled at this. No wonder she felt ready for everything all the time, with that dark circle ever-present, hovering to protect her with love and the defiance of talk at home.

"Celie, dear…? Is everything all right?" Mrs. Browne-Thorne. The lady of the house. Fluttering around her now like her nick-name. "Birdie" Browne-Thorne, the hostess of the Celie Harris Imperial Daughters' Tea.

Celie looked into that figure of ivory lace and dove-grey watered silk and considered the question.

Is everything all right? Well, let's see now. Yes, she was Celie Harris, Halifax's own international songstress of the operatic stage. Yes, she was here by invitation. Yes, she was seated at tea in this Southend parlour-shrine of oak and velvet affluence. There were no more yesses.

No one had come near the small, dark woman since her arrival. Oh, she had been shown into the tea-room, the parlour by her hostess, and seated comfortably enough. The tea-cup was of adequately fine China and the tea-cakes sufficiently dainty, with their companion crustless and anaemic cucumber finger sandwiches, all by her side. The perfect Southend Halifax formal tea picture. Except that not one of the Imperial Daughters had spoken to their dusky guest of honour since her arrival. Instead, they fluttered among themselves, just out of reach. A corner of the storm and flurry of fine lace and brocade and the patina of old pearls against white throats.

Celie raised her eyes to Mrs. Browne-Thorne's uncertain gaze. No words came.

"Fine, dear. Fine. Fine." The bird-like flutter of hands at the crêpey throat. She fled. Back to the reluctant flock, so Celie thought.

Why had they asked her here if they weren't wanting to talk to her? But Celie knew even before the thought was complete. She knew only too well how high her stock was on the social register; at least her name was. Celie Harris, Black girl out of Halifax who sings for Europe and for crowned heads of state and even fills Carnegie Hall with her strong and dusky voice. Celie knew that here at home her name was the prize on the invitation that would be multiplied in the weekend Gazetteer. Her name was of sufficient credit that it would shore up Birdie Browne-Thorne's Southend status. Her name was fine. It was the flag that bannered her art, her music, her song, her celebrity.

Another shadow approaching now. Celie immediately let out that breath from deep in her chest as she recognized the shadow as Dora Skyke from "out home." Mama had reminded her to keep an eye out for Dora. That Dora would look after her here. After all, this was Dora's "place." Her live-in place with the Browne-Thornes for as long as Celie could remember. And longer.

My, didn't Dora look all crisp and stiff and black and white? Bigger somehow than she looked to Celie at church. Anyway, didn't she just own this place, the way she moved in it? Better than Birdie Browne-Thorne herself.

Bit quiet she was, though, here. None of that hearty head-back bellowing laugh of hers that just rang through the Cheapside Market on the week-end mornings. No big "Hey, you-gal!" from Dora in this room. Just that efficient black shadow coming and going. Celie was glad just to see her in that room anyway, that seemed to be growing bigger by the minute.

Dora caught Celie's eye just then and the two women looked closely and warmly into each other, and each felt at home in the other's gaze. Celie caught Dora's broad smile, flashing those gaps in front, and she purely did feel better, almost herself again.

Funny, but she'd wondered and, yes, even worried over knowing she would see Dora here. Celie thought for sure she'd be feeling all hot and just awful at this moment, when Dora would be handing her tea and cakes and looking after her as if she was white. She didn't want to have that happen, but of course it did... the thing was, though, Celie felt all right there with Dora. Dora wasn't feeling at all bad about it. Celie could tell. And at least Dora wasn't pretending that she wasn't there.

Dora was gone. Not really. Just being a shadow again. Black and silent and efficient, bearing tea-cakes to and fro among the Imperial Daughters.

There they all were. Fluffed into clumps and clusters on the settees and such around the perimeter of this room. The talk was low and strained. Well-coiffed heads dipped to shield eyes that stole her way to take the measure of Celie and to record — incredulously — her presence in that pre World War Two room among Halifax gentlewomen.

That clock ticked like a wanton heartbeat.

Celie sat and stiffened and felt her throat; her lovely, lovely throat of musical miracles constrict.

"Why am I here? Why did I come to this farce of a tea? Do they want me here? They want my name. Why don't they talk to me? Ask me something — anything. About Europe. About Carnegie Hall. Anything."

Ah, but Celie knew. They wanted her name. On the social page. High up. Listed conspicuously with theirs. Imperial Daughters of Halifax had Celie Harris to tea as the guest of Mrs. Birdie Browne-Thorne of Young Avenue.

Celie doesn't remember the afternoon ending, or how she got out of there. But she does remember the warm and secret hug from Dora as she put Celie into her coat; and that hot, breathy whisper into Celie's collar, " I knows 'em, child. I knows 'em too well."

The story that Celie took home to her Mama was an artful fabrication of the gaiety of the afternoon, the talks and the camaraderie that she had been drawn into. Mama Harris was happy with that story. Celie's celebrated throat ached and burned while she told it. All lies. And then it was forgotten. Put away where it couldn't trip her as she continued on the exquisite road to acclaim for her voice — the acclaim that was to be hers, both afar and at home, long after that incredible afternoon.

Years later, Celie heard that Dora had left her live-in place with Birdie Browne-Thorne. Quit was the story that Dora told whenever pressed. But there is always something else.

Seems that one of the dowagers of the deep Southend proclaimed to all and sundry that afternoon that, celebrated songstress or not, she could barely abide being to tea with "that gal." And how could Birdie Browne? In fact, as she said or boasted. "It was all I could do to keep from asking that gal to go down to the cellar to fetch a scuttle of coal."

Well it seems that the wrong ears heard; Dora's of course. It also seems that the lady in question went home with coal dust dumped liberally — somehow — into the folds and recesses of her wraps. And once the story got told at the Cheapside Market, complete with mime and that trademark head-thrown-back laugh, Dora soon left Birdie Browne-Thorne's service.

Knowing that years later, Celie allowed the memories of that awful tea party to come back at odd moments; especially in those tight moments before she stepped into some spotlight to open that sweet and dusky throat.

The memories are strong and urgent and filled with Dora's smile and with the ticking heartbeat of the clock in that genteel room.

1990

In Service II

In Service. I grew up hearing those words. As a little girl in my mother's kitchen, I would hear those words. In Service.

"She went in Service."

With little-girl ears where they shouldn't be, bent to lady-talk. That scary, hushed exciting lady-talk between my mother and women who came to see her. Tea and talk. Lady-talk.

In Service, Mama and Miss Riley. Mama and Aunt Lil. Mama and Helen. Helen. The one grown-up person we were allowed to say the name of without a Miss or Aunt in front. Helen. I love to say her name and feel her velvet hats. Tams. She always chewed Juicy Fruit gum.

FIRE ON THE WATER

It was always the same. Talk of dark mysterious women-things, softly spoken. Lips would burble tea in cups. Eyes would roll slowly or point sharply when certain things were said, names were named. Sometimes talk of Mama's In service memories; of her grandmother, a ten-year-old girl being sent in from the country, from Preston, to be In Service. Talk of Aunt Lil, and sometimes with her. Laughing Aunt Lil, with hair like fleeting movie star dreams. Aunt Lil who always included laughing in her lady-talk. And Miss Riley, who never did.

These conversations always seemed to carry their own colours. This one, scary, smoky black, light misty grey. Lady-talk. "Children should be seen and not heard." "Keep in a child's place." I was afraid of those hard, red sentences Mama always had ready during lady-talk. I had to go where they couldn't see me. But in a small house, the scary grey black mist of lady-talk can always find you.

In Service. Sterling silver, glowing in the dark and sunlight words to me. Like the lone brass button always at the bottom of Mama's button box, when I would sneak the polish to it, to bring back the shine. The Mysteries of In Service were all confused and glowing with parade dreams and uniforms marching by in a flash of things shiny and formal.

"Yes, girl, she went In Service when she was ten."

"It was right after I went In Service that Uncle Willy died."

"She was In Service for years."

"She died In Service."

My little-girl mind imagined shiny, wonderful things, not clearly defined. Not knees sore from years on hardwood floors. Not hands cracked, dry and painful, calloused and scrubworn. Not early morning walking miles into town to start the day off right with morning labours for some family. Not always going to and coming from the back door. Not "speak when you're spoken to," see and don't see, hear and don't hear, in case you anger them and they let you go. Not eating their leftovers in the kitchen alone. Not one dollar a day for backbreaking floors, walls, dishes, furniture, windows, washing, ironing, sweat-soaked labour. In Service.

"She died In Service." That describes Helen. I was allowed to say her name. Velvet tams and Juicey Fruit gum every night in Mama's kitchen. When I was little, I was allowed to stand by her and feel her tams. When I got older, she'd be there very night, watching me cry into cold dishwater.

And still the tams were there. The ruby, the emerald green, the midnight velvet blue of them glowed richly against the grey-black, soft, and wooly head. Sometimes she would reach up, too, to finger that soft glow; almost as if to make sure that lovely part of her was still there. Helen's hands against such splendid velvet were like wounds; flags of the world of drudgery that were her days.

Helen was someone's girl, this never married Black lady, already in middle age by the time I was old enough to know her. Somebody's girl. Not in the romantic notion of being somebody's girl (friend). Helen was some white lady's girl; some white family's girl. She came to our house very night as if it was a target; an end point to her day; to sit in our kitchen with a cup of tea; to read the paper. She never took her coat off.

The lady-talk would start. Mama and Helen. It was always about Helen's lady—the woman she worked for. "My family," "My Missus."

Helen "lived In Service," which added to the mystique of it all. My little-girl mind imagined something with a faint glow. Not a room off the back. Not living away from your family. In a house, a bed that was never yours.

Through my window, I could see "Helen's house" not far from my own. On Sunday walks with one or other of my older sisters, seeing "Helen's house" was to see a dream, or at least a story-book page. "Helen's house," huge and golden yellow, with a fence and a yard that held what, in later, grown up years, I would know as a gazebo. But then, surely, that wonderful little in-the-yard house was where she lived, behind cool, dark green lattice.[15] Helen's house. So different from my own, so squat and brown and hen-like. My house, teeming with the dozen of us. My house, that Helen fled to each night; to maybe, for a little while, be a little of what my mother was, and did and had. Mama, with hands on her own dishes; on her own child.

Helen had eyes that were always friendly. I would see them peek behind her tam, even as she sat, and sipped her tea, and waited for it all to happen every night. Waited in the wake of the dark and tiny storm of activity that hummed along after Mama; a whirl-wind of shooing the creeping horde of us.; of moving through clouds of flour from baking; of ironing, or putting up late supper for Daddy; of watching and listening for Daddy; and finally settling down to braid my hair and have tea and lady-talk.

Sometimes Helen would bring a shopping bag full of clothes with her to show Mama. Clothes—castoff, not new—that her lady had given her. Clothes and hats. Velvet tams. Helen. Mama and Helen and lady-talk.

What did a little Black girl know, touching a velvet tam over hooded and frightened eyes? Helen. Perhaps she knew and feared the loneliness of her own life, circled round and round her like an echo; loneliness circled round and worn close, fitting her like the coats and tams from her shopping bag. Perhaps the secret mystery and the fear should hide deep in her eyes from me; from my little-girl eyes watching Helen bring the secret of In Service each night. This world, this life, this loneliness all too real for her. A dark and female mystery still for me.

FIRE ON THE WATER

Helen. Driven like a magnet to somebody else's kitchen; somebody else's child. Helen. With care-worn hands, handing me the future luxury of dreams, and thoughts, and "I remember Helen," and the awful mystery of In Service unravelled now from the whispers of lady-talk, found now in the voice of these words.

Looking back, I know she was saving me. They all were. Helen. Mama. Miss Riley. Aunt Lil. My sisters. Known and unknown Black women. Armies of Black women in that sea of domestic service. With unlikely and unowned addresses. Waiting for buses on prestigious street corners. Carrying back bits and remnants of that other world of In Service in shopping bags; and wearing the rest in coats and velvet tams.

1987

Notes
1. From 1973 to 1989, Chile was ruled by a brutal military dictatorship.
2. In 1979, Nicaraguans revolted against a U.S.-backed dictator and established a popular government, which was then, during the 1980s, attacked by U.S.-backed "Contra" guerillas.
3. Northern Ireland has been torn by Catholic-Protestant sectarian strife.
4. Johannesburg is a major city in South Africa, a state which has rigidly oppressed its Black majority population.
5. Portia White (1911-1968), of Truro, was a contralto and music teacher. Debuted at New York's Town Hall in 1944; gave Command Performance before Queen Elizabeth II in 1964. Famed for her *bel canto* technique, she sang in English, French, German, and Spanish, and recited both spirituals and classical songs.
6. Edith Irene (Drummond) Clayton (1920-1989), of East Preston, was an internationally acclaimed basket weaver. In recognition of her artistry, she was awarded a medal by Queen Elizabeth II in 1977.
7. Graham Norman Jarvis [Cromwell] (1953-1985), of Weymouth Falls, was shot in the thigh and bled to death on a road in Digby County on June 8, 1985. An all-white jury acquitted Jarvis's killer of manslaughter, thus sparking accusations of racism. See George Elliott Clarke, "The Birmingham of Nova Scotia," *New Maritimes*, Vol. 4, Nos. 4-5, pp.4-7.
8. An Algonquian tribe native to Nova Scotia, New Brunswick, and parts of Quebec, Newfoundland, and New England.
9. Kwakiutl or Kwakwaka'wakw is the name of several British Columbia coastal tribes who speak dialects of Kwakwala.
10. A confederacy of five Iroquoian-speaking tribes native to northern Simcoe County, Ontario.
11. Watered silk.
12. Imperial Order of the Daughters of the Empire, an English- Canadian women's social organization.
13. New England.
14. Wrinkled.
15. Structure of cross laths with interstices, serving as screen, door, etc.

Sylvia Hamilton
1950-

Our Mothers Grand and Great: Black Women of Nova Scotia

Very little of what one reads about Nova Scotia would reveal the existence of an Afro-Nova Scotian population that dates back three centuries. Provincial advertising, displays, and brochures reflect people of European ancestry: the Scots, the Celts, the French, and the Irish, among others. There is occasional mention of Nova Scotia's first people, the Micmac. Yet Afro-Nova Scotians live in forty-three communities throughout a province which is populated by over seventy-two different ethnic groups. Tourists and official visitors often express great surprise when they encounter people of African origin who can trace their heritage to the 1700s and 1800s. To understand the lives of Black women in Nova Scotia, one has first to learn something about their people and their environment.

The African presence here began in 1605 when a French colony was established at Port Royal (Annapolis Royal). A Black man, Mathieu da Costa, accompanied Pierre Du Gua, Sieur De Monts, and Samuel de Champlain to the new colony. Da Costa was one of Sieur De Monts's most useful men, as he knew the language of the Micmac and therefore served as interpreter for the French. The existence of Blacks in Nova Scotia remained singular and sporadic until the late 1700s, when three thousand Black Loyalists arrived at the close of the American War of Independence. Though the Black Loyalists were free people, other Blacks who came at the same time with White Loyalists bore the euphemistic title "servant for life." Both groups joined the small population of Black slaves already present in the province. A second major influx of Blacks would occur following the War of 1812; approximately two thousand former slaves, the Black Refugees, arrived in Nova Scotia during the postwar period between 1813 and 1816.

African people have a long tradition of oral history; stories about their heroes and heroines have therefore gone unrecorded. When a people begins the process of creating a written record of their champions, an initial tendency is to lionize and revere all. Since they will be paraded for all to see, faults and shortcomings are minimized and criticism is not often tolerated. The making of cultural heroes and heroines is an act of unification and empowerment. This process, just beginning among Afro-Nova Scotians, is integral to the survival of a people.

> On Saturday next, at twelve o'clock, will be sold on the Beach, two hogshead of rum, three of sugar, and two well-grown negro girls, aged fourteen and twelve, to the highest bidder.

From her first arrival in Nova Scotia, the Black woman has been immersed in a struggle for survival. She has had to battle slavery, servitude, sexual and racial discrimination, and ridicule. Her tenacious spirit has been her strongest and most constant ally; she is surviving with a strong dignity and an admirable lack of self-pity and bitterness. She is surviving, but not without struggle.

During Nova Scotia's period of slavery, Black female slaves were called upon to do more than simple domestic chores for their masters. Sylvia was a servant of Colonel Creighton of Lunenburg. On July 1, 1782, the town was invaded by soldiers from the strife-ridden American Colonies. Sylvia shuttled cartridges hidden in her apron from Creighton's house to the fort where he was doing battle. When the house came under fire, Sylvia threw herself on top of the Colonel's son to protect him. During the battle she also found time to conceal her master's valuables in a bag which she lowered into the well for safekeeping. Typically, it was not Sylvia who was recognized for her efforts, but her master and a militia private to whom the provincial House of Assembly voted payments of money from the county's land taxes.

Another tidy arrangement involved slave-holding ministers. These men of the cloth adjusted their beliefs and principles accordingly when they purchased slaves. Lunenburg's Presbyterian minister John Secombe kept a journal in which he noted that "Dinah, my negro woman-servant made a profession and confession publickly (sic) and was baptized, July 17, 1774." Dinah had a son, Solomon, who was brought to the province as a slave and who died in 1855 at age ninety; no record was found of the date of Dinah's death. In 1788 a mother and daughter were enslaved by Truro's Presbyterian pastor, Reverend Daniel Cock. When the mother became "unruly," he sold her but kept the daughter. In the same year, a Black woman named Mary Postill was sold in Shelburne; her price was one hundred bushels of potatoes.

Many slaves could hold no hope of being set free upon the death of their owners. Annapolis merchant Joseph Totten left his wife Suzannah the use of "slaves, horses, cattle, stock etc." and "to each of three daughters a negro girl slave...to her executors, administrators and assigns for ever." Amen. Others who were not given their freedom seized it for themselves. Determined owners placed newspaper ads offering rewards for their return.

SYLVIA HAMILTON

While Black women slaves were being sold, left in wills, traded, and otherwise used, Black Loyalist women, ostensibly free, endeavoured to provide a livelihood for themselves and their families while at the same time labouring to establish communities. In 1787 Catherine Abernathy, a Black Loyalist teacher, instructed children in Preston, near Halifax. She taught a class of twenty children in a log schoolhouse built by the people of the community. Abernathy established a tradition of Black women teachers which would be strongly upheld by her sisters in years to come. Similarly, her contemporaries Violet King and Phillis George, the wives of ministers, carved another distinct path: Black women supporting their men and at the same time providing a stable base for their families. Even though history has documented the lives of David George[1] and Boston King,[2] it has remained silent on the experiences of Violet and Phillis.

What must it have been like for Phillis George in Shelburne in the late 1780s? Her husband travelled extensively, setting up Baptist churches in Nova Scotia and New Brunswick. He preached to and baptized Blacks and Whites alike, not a popular undertaking at that time. The Georges had three children; money and food were scarce. On one occasion, a gang of fifty former soldiers armed with a ship's tackle surrounded their household, overturning it and what contents it had. Some weeks later, on a Sunday, a mob arrived at George's church; they whipped and beat him, driving the Baptist minister into the swamps of Shelburne. Under the cover of darkness, David George made his way back to town, collected Phillis and the children, and fled to neighbouring Birchtown.

What of Phillis George and other Black Loyalist women: unnamed women who were weavers, seamstresses, servants, bakers, and hat makers? We can in some measure recreate the society they lived in; we can even speculate on what they looked like. But except for isolated cases, their memories and experiences are their own and will remain with them, fixed in time.

One of those rare, isolated instances is that of Rose Fortune. A descendant of the Black Loyalists, Rose lived in Annapolis Royal in the mid-1880s. She distinguished herself by establishing a baggage service for travellers arriving by boat at Annapolis from Saint John and Boston. A modest wheelbarrow and her strong arms were her two biggest assets. Rose's noteworthy activities were not only commercial. She concerned herself with the well-being of the young and old alike. Rose Fortune declared herself policewoman of the town and as such took upon herself the responsibility of making sure young children were safely off the streets at night. Her memory is kept alive by her descendants, the Lewis family of Annapolis Royal. Daurene Lewis[3] is an accomplished weaver whose work is well known in Nova

Scotia. She also holds the distinction of being the first Black woman elected to a town council in the province.

Black Loyalists had been promised land sufficient to start new lives in Nova Scotia. However, when the grants of land were allocated, the Black Loyalists received much less than their White counterparts. Dissatisfaction with this inequity coupled with an unyielding desire to build a better future for their families and provided the impetus for an exodus to Sierra Leone, West Africa, where the Black Loyalists hoped life would be different. In 1792 Phillis and David George, along with twelve hundred Black Loyalists, sailed from Nova Scotia to Sierra Leone.

Four years later, five hundred Jamaican Maroons were sent in exile to Nova Scotia. A proud people, the Maroons were descendants of runaway slaves who for over one hundred fifty years waged war against the British colonists in Jamaica. Upon their arrival, the men were put to work on reconstruction of Citadel Hill. Of the Maroon women, very little is recorded. We do know they were used for the entertainment of some of the province's esteemed leaders: Governor John Wentworth is believed to have taken a Maroon woman as his mistress, while Alexander Ochterloney, a commissioner placed in charge of the Maroons, "took five or six of the most attractive Maroon girls to his bed, keeping what the surveyor of Maroons, Theophilus Chamberlain, called a 'seraglio for his friends.'" The Maroon interlude ended in 1800 when they too set sail for Sierra Leone.

Between 1813 and 1816 the Black Refugees made their way to the province. It is this group whose memory is strongest in Nova Scotia, for their descendants may be found in communities such as Hammonds Plains, Preston, Beechville, Conway, Cobequid Road, and Three Mile Plains. Some of the earliest sketches and photographs of the Halifax city market show Black women selling baskets overflowing with mayflowers. Basketweaving for them was not an activity used to fill idle time: it was work aimed at bringing in money vital to the survival of the family. This century-old tradition has endured because there are women who learned the craft from their mothers, who in turn learned it from their mothers. Edith Clayton[4] of East Preston has been weaving maple market baskets since she was eight years old; it is a tradition which reaches back to touch six generations of her family. Not only does Edith Clayton continue to make and sell baskets, she also teaches classes in basketweaving throughout Nova Scotia as a means of preserving and passing on a significant and uniquely Afro-Nova Scotian aspect of the culture and heritage of the province.

Many and varied are the roles Black women have played and continue to play within their own and the broader community. It has often been said they are the backbone of the Black community:

organizers, fund-raisers, nurturers, care-givers, mourners. When an attempt was made in 1836 by the provincial government to send the people of Preston to Trinidad, it was the women who objected:

> They all appear fearful of embarking on the water —many of them are old and have large families, and if a few of the men should be willing to go, the Women would not. It is objected among them that they have never heard any report of those who were sent away a few years ago to the same place, and think that if they were doing well some report of it would have reached them. They seem to have some attachment to the soil they have cultivated, poor and barren as it is...

Nowhere has their involvement been more pronounced than in the social, educational, and religious life of the Black community. In 1917 the women of the African Baptist churches in the province gathered together to establish a Ladies' Auxiliary which would take responsibility for the "stimulation of the spiritual, moral, social, educational, charitable, and financial work of all the local churches of the African Baptist Association."

These women gathered outside around a well in the community of East Preston since the church had no space for them to use; this gathering became known as the "Women of the Well." Some of these same women later organized an auxiliary to provide support for the Nova Scotia Home for Coloured Children. In 1920, for the first time in Canadian history, a Convention of Coloured Women was held in Halifax.

A woman well-respected throughout Nova Scotia's Black community is ninety-four-year-old Muriel V. States.[5] She was present on that day the women gathered at the well to establish the Ladies' Auxiliary. She was present as well at another historic event: the 1956 creation of the Women's Institute of the Ladies' Auxiliary she had helped to organize thirty-nine years before.

One hundred five delegates were registered for a meeting whose theme was "Building Better Communities." Among the issues discussed were community health and educational standards and family relations. Muriel States, who was the Auxiliary's Official Organizer at the time, told her sisters their activities would not go unnoticed:

> Today, we women of the African Baptist Association have taken another step which will go down in history as the first Women's Institute held this day at this church. We feel that we as women have accomplished much and are aiming to do great things in the future. We are already reaping the reward of untiring and united effort in all that tends to the promotion of the church and community welfare.

Since 1956 the meeting of the Women's Institute has been an annual event. In October, 1981, the Institute celebrated its twenty-fifth anniversary. Its history tells of the dedicated work of many women: Gertrude Smith, Margaret Upshaw, Pearleen Oliver,[6] Selina David, Catherine Clarke, and many others.

Today the Institute undoubtedly records the largest gatherings of Black women in the province; annual conventions draw several hundred Black women.

In 1937 the Nova Scotia Teachers' College in Truro had a student population of over one hundred students. My mother Marie[7] remembers being one of the college's two Black students; her companion was Ada Symonds. Teaching was my mother's second choice for a career; nursing, her first choice, was not open to Blacks. The bar remained solidly across this door until 1945, when pressure from the Nova Scotia Association for the Advancement of Coloured People and from Reverend William[8] and Pearleen Oliver forced its removal. Two Black women were admitted as trainees in nursing.

Teaching became the selected profession for many Black women. Some chose it because they wanted to teach, others because there were no other options open. These women are remembered in the many communities where they taught. They are especially remembered for their diligent work and commitment in the face of the hardship and adversity of a society which has tried unceasingly to deny their existence. They had to put up with one-room segregated schools, few resources, and little money. They stayed late to devote extra time to those students who had to stay home to help pick blueberries and mayflowers or to help garden. When the school day was over, another day began for them: seeing to their own children, cooking supper, ironing the children's clothes for school, preparing lessons, and attending a meeting at the church.

As they laboured at teaching, nursing, housekeeping, typing, and other jobs, Black women have not led easy lives. Nova Scotian Black women, like their counterparts elsewhere, have always known a double day. Some say the Black woman invented it. Work was and continues to be an integral part of her life. She has not had the luxury of deciding to stay home; with the current state of both our provincial and national economies, it is unlikely she will be afforded that choice in the near future.

Public attention in Canada has been increasingly riveted upon incidents of racially motivated attacks on individuals and groups in some of our major urban centres. The manner in which these cases have been described would lead one to believe such occurrences are relatively new phenomena in this country. Even the most cursory examination of the experiences of Afro-Nova Scotians will clearly demonstrate that, indeed, such is not the case.

In 1946 New Glasgow theatres were segregated; Blacks sat upstairs, Whites occupied the downstairs seats. While in New Glasgow, Viola Desmond of Halifax decided to go to the theatre. She bought a ticket (balcony seat) but decided to sit downstairs. Though she was ordered to move, Viola refused, offering instead to pay the difference in price. The theatre manager declined the offer and called the police. Viola Desmond was carried away by the officer and held in jail overnight. The next day she was fined twenty dollars and costs. She was charged with having avoided paying the one-cent entertainment tax. A year later, Selma Burke, a Black woman from the United States, was refused service in Halifax. It is not difficult to see that this environment had the power to dampen spirits, damage identities, and lessen the desire for change. But there were Black women who felt equal to the challenge.

A New Glasgow publishing venture which began as an eight-by-ten broadside in 1945 soon blossomed into a full-fledged newspaper. This was *The Clarion*, edited and published by Dr. Carrie Best.[9] Published twice monthly, *The Clarion* called itself the voice of "coloured Nova Scotians." Dr. Best published timely articles on civil-rights issues in Nova Scotia and elsewhere; the paper featured a women's page and carried sports and social news. In 1949 *The Clarion* gave birth to *The Negro Citizen*, which achieved nationwide circulation. But Dr. Best was not moving down a totally untravelled path; one century before, in 1853, Mary Shadd Cary launched *The Provincial Freeman* from Windsor, Ontario. In so doing, she became the first Black woman in North America to found and edit a weekly newspaper. Dr. Best has been awarded the Order of Canada; in 1977 she published her autobiography, *That Lonesome Road*.

Other Black flowers were blossoming as well in the 1940s. When Portia White[10] was seventeen she was teaching school and taking singing lessons. Winning the Silver Cup at the Nova Scotia Music Festival paved the way for her to receive a scholarship from the Halifax Ladies Musical Club to study at the Halifax Conservatory of Music. By the time she was thirty-one, Portia White had made her musical debut in Toronto. Four years later, in 1945, she made her debut at New York's famed Town Hall and later toured the United States and Europe. Of the "young Canadian contralto's" debut, one New York critic wrote:

> as soon as she stepped on to the stage and began to sing it was obvious that here was a young musician of remarkable talents. Miss White has a fine, rich voice which she uses both expressively and intelligently ... The artist has an excellent stage presence ... she was greeted with enthusiastic applause at each entrance. Miss White is a singer to watch, a singer with a bright future.

In 1969 Portia White's estate donated a gift of one thousand dollars to the Halifax City Regional Library to assist in setting up a music library in the city. The record collection which was subsequently installed is large and varied; few members of the borrowing public, however, know how the collection they so enjoy was originally established.

Recently Black women in Nova Scotia have begun to enter areas where their absence has heretofore been conspicuous: government, law, journalism, business, and medicine. This is not to say the struggle has ended or that we have arrived. While the attitude of the Black woman toward herself has been undergoing changes, the perceptions and attitudes of others both within her own community and beyond it require continual challenges to bring about any significant changes in how she is regarded and treated by others. As Black women begin paying tribute to themselves and their own work, others will pay tribute also. This year the family of Joyce Ross, a daycare director and long-standing community worker in East Preston, held a recognition dinner in her honour. Pearleen Oliver, author, historian, and educator, was one of three women selected to receive the YWCA Recognition of Women Award initiated in 1981. She was the first woman to serve as moderator of the African United Baptist Association and is the author of *Brief History of Colored Baptists of Nova Scotia 1782-1953* (1953), and *A Root and a Name* (1977). When the Recognition of Women Award was announced for 1982, Doris Evans, an educator and community worker, was among the three women honoured. And there are still many others who have experiences that need to be examined and stories that need to be told — women such as Ada Fells of Yarmouth, Edith Cromwell of Bridgetown, Clotilda Douglas of Sydney, Elsie Elms of Guysborough, Ruth Johnson of Cobequid Road. And there are others...

Writer Mary Helen Washington, in the introduction to her book *Midnight Birds*, speaks of the process whereby Black women recover and rename their past. She talks about the monuments and statues erected by White men to celebrate their achievements and "to remake history, and to cast themselves eternally in heroic form." Yet there is no trace of women's lives. "We have," she says, "been erased from history." As research and exploration into the lives of Black women in Nova Scotia continues, a fuller view, one with dimension and perspective, will emerge. We will know then where to erect our monument. Now there are only signposts pointing the way.

1982

Potato Lady

dusty brown potato
white eyes protruding
she turns it in
her hand, knife poised
and thinks

of Mary Postill[11]
sold
for a bushel of potatoes

1992

Garden Picnic at Meadowbank (P. E. I.)

White swans and yellow ducks
Black ceramic people
on white and blue
ceramic benches
They sit properly in twos
(neatly mowed green grass underfoot)
among assorted animals—
all silent
as if waiting for a cue to begin.

1986

Untitled

Cocoa brown cattails
standing erect
asleep in fields
of powder white snow
waiting to be awakened by Spring.
Birds pass quickly:
no messages.

1986

FIRE ON THE WATER

These People who Do Business with the Dead

These men who make their business burying the dead
Black, shiny, ill-fitting jackets
wrinkled, almost by design
Pinstriped pants, white gloves
almost always too large
Sombre white countenances
accompany greasy hair parted
à la 50's styles

They come as rude intruders
who are paid to provide comfort
and to take care of things
Like human ASA[12] they
(remove worries) and headaches

So familiar are those faces
yet only one, his, the Undertaker's is
truly familiar
Seen many times before

Let them not call him for me.

1992

Ladies on the Number 3

faded green trench coat
worn, wrinkled black hands
wedding band no longer fits.
she talks quietly, so softly to herself
on the bus in the rain.
her black leather purse
old and wearing thin,
its side pockets bulging:
in one, wild cherrydrops,
the other, old letters —
bundles of old letters.

1985

Sleet and Glass

She said it was chunks of broken glass.
Don't be foolish, they told her.
It's only sleet, go.
Still not believing, she left,
Walked onto the deck.
As more pieces fell around her
she looked down at her bare brown feet
as the blood began to flow
then over her shoulder
to the windows where
they stood (wearing confident smiles)
watching her.
She wondered what she saw in their eyes.

1986

In My Neighbourhood

In my neighbourhood
the wind blows in from the bay

Small purple wildflowers
idly watch from the roadside

Blackberries sun themselves
turning their fat bodies toward the sky

(or, blackberries glisten, sun themselves,
turning their fat bodies toward the sky)

In my neighbourhood
they sprayed KKK[13] in black
on my mailbox

Down the road a piece
a black jockey
from earlier times
remains on guard,
even in winter.

In my neighbourhood
nobody wants to
know my secrets.

1992

FIRE ON THE WATER

Facing My Own Poverty

In Matanzas[14] —
small houses set upon
narrow sidewalks
doors open wide, or a crack
Many faces in each room
some sad
others stare out
with curious eyes
Black faces too
I face my past

My camera stops
on its way to my eyes
I fear what will be
reflected in the lens
Small, Black and dusty girl
short dress, ashen legs
long braided black hair
looking down a rocky hill
at the car below
White faces peer upwards
cameras wedged between us
they don't come out of the car
Taking pictures of poverty

Now, I look from a distance
through my 135mm lens
They may not see me
Now, Black looks at black
and finds no comfort
Later, I see clothes
strung out on a rope line
a slender, branchless tree
a prop, to hold up the line

And Where am I?

1992

Notes
1. David George (c.1743-1810), a Baptist Black Loyalist leader. His work appears in this anthology.
2. Boston King (1760-1802), a Methodist Black Loyalist leader. His work appears in this anthology.
3. Daurene Lewis was mayor of Annapolis Royal from 1984 to 1988.

4. Edith Irene (Drummond) Clayton (1920-1989), of East Preston, was an internationally acclaimed basket weaver. For her skill in this traditional Africadian craft, she was awarded a medal by Queen Elizabeth II in 1977.
5. Muriel V. States (1888-1984), born in Avonport, wed Rev. Wellington Naey States (1877-1927) in 1907. Served 40 years as official organizer of the Ladies Auxiliary of the AUBA. Was also a supervisor of children at the Nova Scotia Home for Coloured Children.
6. Dr. Pearleen Oliver (1917-) assisted her husband, Rev. Dr. W.P. Oliver, to teach and lead Africadians. A historian, her work appears in this anthology.
7. Dr. Marie Hamilton (1912-), of Halifax, a teacher and community worker. She is the mother of Sylvia Hamilton, whose work appears in this anthology.
8. Rev. Dr. William Pearly Oliver (1912-1989) worked with and inspired Africadians in the fields of religion, education, and human rights. His work appears in this anthology.
9. Dr. Carrie M. Best (1903-), of New Glasgow, is a journalist, historian, and human rights advocate. Her work appears in this anthology.
10. Portia White (1911-1968), of Truro, was a contralto and music teacher. Debuted at New York's Town Hall in 1944; gave Command Performance before Queen Elizabeth II in 1964. Famed for her *bel canto* technique, she sang in four languages, and recited both spirituals and classical songs.
11. In the 1780s, Jesse Gray, of Argyle, had sold to William Maugham, of Shelburne, Mary Postill, for 100 bushels of potatoes. See Thomas Watson Smith, "The Loyalists at Shelburne," *Nova Scotia Historical Society, Collections,* VI (1889) p.75.
12. Acetylsalicylic acid, also called aspirin.
13. Ku Klux Klan, a secret society founded in 1866 in Pulaski, Tennessee. It sought to terrorize the newly-freed Blacks into submission through assault and murder. The KKK preaches hatred of Blacks, Jews, Catholics, and liberals.
14. Matanzas, Cuba

George Boyd
1952-

Consecrated Ground
A Teleplay

Prologue

Nestled along the shores of Halifax's Bedford Basin, Africville was a small, black settlement of nearly 400 residents.

Although the village was within its boundaries, the City did not provide Africville with basic services. There was no water, electricity[1] or sewage. A dump was situated just 350 feet from the settlement.

In the early 1960's, the City began to expropriate the land and relocate the residents of Africville.

Many residents of Africville fought the move, contending decisions were being made arbitrarily and without fair consultation.

The following is a fictional dramatization of one aspect of their story....

1. EXT. AFRICVILLE. DAY

It is winter; wind howling, an infant crying. We hear the hymn, *MY FATHER'S HOUSE*. The opening shot reveals a landscape that is bleak, barren and painted in dull tones of grey against dirt-tinted snow.

Opening credits roll.

SUPER: AFRICVILLE, 1966

As the camera pans, we see a small, unimposing church in the background. This is from where the hymn emanates. The camera pulls back to reveal a small shack. CLARICE is kneeling with a water bucket beside an outdoor well. She is pumping the well vigorously, but only a trickle of water pours out. She's obviously underestimated the intensity of the weather, as she's clad in only a housecoat and a pair of old boots.

CUT TO:

A tight shot of CLARICE'S hands chipping away at the ice that's clogged the water sprout. She halts, catches her breath, and starts pumping the well again. A nearby sign reads: CONTAMINATED WATER: BOIL BEFORE DRINKING.

The infant's crying is louder. Clarice calls his name, as if to comfort him from a distance.

CLARICE:
Momma's comin', Tully. Momma's comin. I'm just gettin' some water for your formula, baby, Momma's.... comin'...

Tully's wailing intensifies, builds to a cresendo, then suddenly stops.

Clarice turns her head to the house. She cocks her head but hears only the desolate silence of the howling wind, the faint, lilting hymn.

CLARICE:
Tully?...

She gets to her feet, stands, looking in the direction of the house.

CLARICE:
(Louder now) Tully?...

She starts walking rapidly towards the house.

CLARICE:
Tully?...

She breaks into a full run. A heartbeat pounds faintly at first, then increases in intensity.

2. INT. KITCHEN/BEDROOM. DAY.

She runs through the back door and into the kitchen, knocking over whatever is in her way. As she runs into Tully's bedroom, she sees a shadow dart from the top of his crib.

Rats scurry.

She stops, motionless. In her terror, she cannot move. She can't catch her breath, even to utter a word.

A rat runs between her legs.

She screams, running to the crib. She sees TULLY and her eyes drain of life. Her mouth forms a scream, but there is no sound.

She snatches Tully from his crib, clutches him in her arms and swaddles him in his blood-stained blanket. Barely audible, she calls her husband's name (WILLEM) as she runs from the house and out into the frozen yard.

3. EXT. YARD. DAY.

She trips and falls in the snow. Screaming for help, she scrambles to her feet.

CLARICE:
Somebody help me.... help me...Willem...

She runs towards the church.

FIRE ON THE WATER

* * *

5. EXT. A FIELD. DAY.

In the distance, CLARICE falls into the snow. The heartbeat stops. As WILLEM approaches her, he drops to his knees, tries to help her, but he cannot move her.

WILLEM:
Clarice? ... 'Leasey? ...

He finally manages to lift her head. He sees TULLY...

WILLEM:
OhmyGod...Tully? ...

SARAH and REVEREND MINER have gathered and stare in horror as they see CLARICE'S blood-soaked housecoat and the swaddled TULLY.

REVEREND MINER:
(To Sarah) I'll get an ambulance.

SARAH:
They won't come.

REVEREND MINER:
The police...I'll call the police.

SARAH:
Reverend...they won't come either! Git them inside.

SARAH goes to WILLEM and CLARICE.

SARAH:
Come on, Willem. We gotta git 'em inside. Git her on her feet. Help 'em, Reverend.

WILLEM:
It gonna be all right, baby...

CLARICE:
He ain't movin', Willem. Tully ain't goin'. Don't take my baby...

REVEREND MINER throws his minister's robes over her shoulders and as they get Clarice to her feet.

BLACKOUT

6. EXT. THE AFRICVILLE DUMP. SUNSET.

The sun is setting on the Bedford Basin horizon. In the foreground is the Africville dump. A rat is perched atop a pile of debris. A bulldozer sits idle to the left.

* * *

11. INT. BEDROOM. EVENING.

Willem looks at Sarah, then at Clarice. He goes to Clarice and gives her an awkward embrace[....]

CLARICE:
Did you tell Reverend Miner what I told ya to tell him?

WILLEM shrugs, unable to answer.

CLARICE:
I said, did you tell Reverend Miner what I told ya to tell 'em?

WILLEM:
Yeah, Leasey. Yeah, I told 'em just what you said.

CLARICE:
And?

WILLEM:
And he said he wants to hold a memorial service for Tully the day after tomorrow.

CLARICE:
That ain't what I'm talking about.

WILLEM:
Now girl you know the Reverend wants to help us, but, well, it ain't entirely in his hands. Mr. Clancy says there's strict laws about—

CLARICE:
Clancy?

WILLEM:
The white man from the city.

CLARICE:
A white man?

WILLEM:
Yes, Clarice, but that don't mean—

CLARICE:
Why you askin' him about Tully? He ain't got no business in this. You should've asked Reverend Miner.

WILLEM:
That's what I'm tryin' to tell you, babe. Mr. Clancy says it is his business. He says the city got laws against what we're askin' and—

CLARICE:
What laws? What kind-a laws say a mother can't bury her baby? (beat) What kind-a laws? (beat) Willem, I askin' you.

Realizing the futility, CLARICE stares away; then.

FIRE ON THE WATER

CLARICE:
Well did you ask this Mister Clancy how he thinks he can stop me from burying my child in Africville?

WILLEM:
I asked him, Leasey. He said they got ordinances and...and by-laws and...he said you got to have a special permit for this! People just can't go round diggin' holes, my—

CLARICE:
Permits? I don't see no permits for them demolishing tractors. And them garbage trucks? They got permits to be movin' people's belongings in garbage trucks?

WILLEM:
Leasey, the man says you gotta have consecrated ground to bury someone. And there ain't no consecrated ground in Africville.

CLARICE:
(In disbelief) No consecrated ground? (long pause; sadness) No consecrated ground...What is Africville if it ain't consecrated ground? This land been in my family for years, Willem, over a hundred years. My ancestors, they consecrated this ground. I watched my Momma and Poppa seed on this ground—till their backs was breakin'. It's...it's where everyone of 'em lived and where they died. And no Mister-Clancy-city-white-man is jumpin' in here and sayin' any different. I know...I saw it...I lived it...Don't he dare tell me there ain't no consecrated ground.

CLARICE runs into the kitchen, grabs WILLEM'S jacket from the chair and throws it at him.

* * *

14. INT. CHURCH. DAY.

WILLEM is standing over TULLY'S coffin. He is alone, distraught. His head is bowed, as if in prayer. The door opens and CLANCY enters.

CLANCY:
Willem?

WILLEM wipes his eyes and turns to him.

CLANCY:
Maybe this is the wrong time. I can come back.

WILLEM:
No, no, come in Mister Clancy. God's house is open to all people.

CLANCY:
He takes a document from his coat.

I just brought that agreement along for you to sign and I'll be on my way.

WILLEM:
Sure, Mister Clancy.

CLANCY walks towards WILLEM. He feels uncomfortable as he nears the casket.

* * *

16. EXT. A FIELD. DAY.

CLARICE is standing in a field overlooking Bedford Basin.

WILLEM, contract in hand, approaches from behind.

WILLEM:
(softly)...Leasey...

CLARICE:
(long pause) Look, Willem.

WILLEM:
What?

CLARICE:
I kin feel 'em, Willem. Just like it was yesterday...I kin feel 'em...

WILLEM:
Babe, it's cold out here, why don't we—

CLARICE:
This is where my Grandmomma and Grandaddy lived...right here on this spot. You standin' in the middle of their livingroom, now, Willem. Grandaddy built their place with his bare hands...and God, I can feel his pride...and his love of his land. Grandaddy died in this field. Died in my Momma's arms ya know...

WILLEM:
I...ah, never knew...

CLARICE:
And Willem? ...

WILLEM:
What, babe?

CLARICE:
This is where our Tully's gonna be buried.

WILLEM:
Leasey...

CLARICE:
Tully gonna be buried right here with his own people. He ain't gonna lie next to strangers.

WILLEM cannot answer. He just looks at her. He stuffs the Quit Claim Deed[2] into his pocket. He kisses her cheek and slowly turns to leave.

17. EXT. THE CHURCH. EVENING.

From a long shot, we see Clancy talking to another (black) man on the steps of the church. CLANCY hands the man a piece of paper. They shake hands and the man leaves. Clancy goes inside.

18. INT. THE CHURCH. EVENING.

CLANCY sitting in one of the pews, puts some papers in his case and snaps it shut. He is about to get up and leave when CLARICE enters. She walks towards the casket, but halts when she sees CLANCY.

CLARICE:
Tully got to be buried in Africville, Reverend.

CLANCY:
Excuse me, you must be Willem's wife. Mrs. Lyle, I'm Tom Clancy, and—

CLARICE:
I ain't here to talk to you. (To Miner) Tully's gonna be buried here. This is where he belongs, Reverend.

REVEREND MINER:
Clarice, do you know why we bury our loved ones in consecrated ground? It's to sanctify the soul. It is to—

CLANCY:
Mrs. Lyle, did your husband explain the city law to you about consecrated land?

CLARICE:
Africville is already consecrated, Mister Clancy. It's your bulldozer around here desecratin' the land, tearin' up people's lives. And you are desecratin' their souls.

CLANCY:
We are relocating residents of Africville so that we may provide people with better living conditions. Do you think those people who have new homes, with running water and electricity—do those people feel they've been desecrated?

CLARICE:
If it hadn't been for the city, Mister Clancy, the people would've had running water and electricity right here. Right here, Mister Clancy.

And the people ain't happy. They're scared of you and yer bulldozers. They're plain scared, and that's why they signed their land away.

CLANCY:

You're missing the point.

CLARICE:

Am I?

CLANCY:

What I'm saying is most people see the benefits of moving. And those who haven't yet moved, don't want their properties devalued by having a cemetery built on their doorsteps. Times have changed, Mrs. Lyle. Society can no longer justify segregation and having people live in substandard conditions. And, people no longer tolerate neighbourhoods just for whites, and ghettos for coloureds. I'm not saying there's no prejudice left, but maybe by the time your children have grown—

CLANCY and MINER exchange glances.

CLARICE:

I ain't got no child, Mister Clancy. You killed him.

CLANCY:

No. We did not kill your child, Mrs. Lyle. We—

CLARICE:

You killed my child. You killed Tully the day you built that dump on our doorsteps. People living here, and your city built homes for rats, then you fed the people's children to them.

CLANCY:

(beat; regains composure) Mrs. Lyle, look, I'm sorry. I truly am sorry about the loss of your child, but I must also inform you that under no circumstances will the city agree to consecrate any land in Africville for your child's burial. Do you understand me? Under no circumstances. I'm sorry.

CLANCY looks at the REVEREND, nods, and leaves.

REVEREND MINER:

Clarice, I—

CLARICE:

Ain't no more to say, is there, Reverend? (long pause) Just...ain't no more to say.

REVEREND MINER embraces her, but she's stiff as a board. Pulling back, he looks at her, and leaves.

19. EXT. THE CHURCH. NIGHT.

FIRE ON THE WATER

CLANCY, having a cigarette, is standing on the steps as the door to the church swings open. CLARICE comes out. She walks past him, he stops her.

CLANCY:

Mrs. Lyle...

CLARICE stops but doesn't turn around.

CLANCY:

There's something I don't understand.

CLARICE:

What?

CLANCY:

If you feel as strongly as you do about this place, why'd you agree to sell your land?

CLARICE turns to him with a look of utter shock. She is about to answer him, when a look of dreaded realization crosses her face.

20. INT. KITCHEN/BEDROOM. NIGHT.

WILLEM is seated at the kitchen table. He's reading the Bible. CLARICE enters, stands in the doorway, trembling in a plethora of different feelings....

CLARICE:

You signed the papers on his casket. ON HIS CASKET!

WILLEM:

I'd have signed them on his grave. I'd have signed them on his goddamned grave if I thought it would get us away from here.

WILLEM grabs her by the arms and pushes her against the wall.

WILLEM:

You stupid bitch. Tully'd be alive if we hadda moved out of here. You stupid, goddamned bitch; he'd be alive.

CLARICE lashes out at him, repeatedly slapping his face.

WILLEM fends off some of the blows as she flails at him.

CLARICE:

Don't...you...call me...don't you...The white man takes advantage of stupid niggers, Willem. And you're a stupid nigger!

WILLEM is finally able to subdue her hands, by wrapping his arms around her. They slump to the floor, exhausted, panting, crying, in embraces and kisses. They weep in each other's arms...

WILLEM:

I did it for us...I just wanted the best for us...

CLARICE:
Don't be ashamed of us, Willem...don't be ashamed...we all they allow us to be...

* * *

21. INT. CHURCH. NIGHT.

The pulpit area is in darkness, lit only by a single incandescent bulb overhanging the cross at the front of the church.

CLARICE is seated in the front pew, a few feet away from Tully's casket. She is holding his blood-stained blanket.

The door at the back of the church opens. Sarah enters and makes her way towards the front. CLARICE does not turn back to look. Sarah takes a place beside Clarice.

The bulldozer starts again.

CLARICE:
They won't stop...won't stop till every trace of Africville is gone; right, Sarah? They gonna make sure nobody ever knew Africville was here, that niggers ever lived here. They gonna make sure there's nothing left of us.

SARAH:
Honey, they been tryin' to be rid of Africville since the first day it was built. They tried everything they could to force us outta here; but, see, the nigger's too smart and agile. The poor got a agility, see, baby. They wouldn't sell to us from their market, so we learned to grow our own food. They wouldn't give us no water, so we dug the well. No 'lectricity, so we made candles and used kerosene...(beat)...No worship in their temples, so we built this church...Baby, if there's one thing we learned, it how to be agile. Guess if you're a nigger in this country, ya got to have agility or you'll perish.

CLARICE:
But, Tully, Sarah, Tully, he was too young to learn all that stuff. Too young to defend his-self.

SARAH:
Guess...what I'm sayin', Leasey, is that they can tear down the buildings, but they never gonna erode our spirit. Africville lives in here(gestures to her heart)...it got to...ain't got no other place to go, now. And you'll see, baby, Tully'll live in here, too.

SARAH squeezes CLARICE'S hand as she rises to leave. CLARICE doesn't watch her go. When she hears the door shut, she goes over to stand by the coffin. Holding the blanket, she simply stares at it.

* * *

23. EXT. FIELD. NIGHT.

CLARICE stands at the same spot in the field as in Scene 16. Clutching Tully in her arms, she sings to him, humming. Throughout this scene, until the end of the play, the sound of the bulldozer can be heard faintly at first, then growing in volume as it gets closer. However, it is never seen.

On a flute, the hymn, *ALL MY TRIALS* is played in the background.

CLARICE kneels to the ground, laying Tully beside her. She begins to dig a grave with her bare hands.

WILLEM & REVEREND MINER approach from behind; yet, CLARICE continues digging. They stand in disbelief and bewilderment, watching her. WILLEM, tears in his eyes, moves towards her, then kneels to face her. Without stopping, CLARICE raises her head to look at him.

He looks into her eyes.

She lowers her head again.

Finally, Willem moves closer to her, helping her dig.

After a moment, Reverend Miner takes out his Bible and begins quietly reading from the Eighth Psalm.

REVEREND MINER:
Out of the mouths of babes and sucklings hast thou ordained strength, oh Lord, because of thine enemies. When mine enemies are turned back, they shall fall and perish at Thy presence. And he shall judge the world in righteousness, he shall minister judgement to the people in uprightness, oh Lord.

The noise of the bulldozer, which is now very close, has almost drowned out the last lines of the Psalm. He continues.

REVEREND MINER:
I do consecrate this holy and sacred ground, and do bless the soul that lies herein to eternal and everlasting life in the name of Jesus Christ Our Lord, Amen.

The camera begins to pull back slowly. We see CLARICE and WILLEM digging, and REVEREND MINER standing beside them. The camera continues to pull back until, in the darkness of night, they can no longer be seen.

BLACKOUT.

SUPER:
In January, 1970, the last resident of Africville was relocated to a city-owned home.

Today, the Africville site contains a park and the approach roads to the A. Murray MacKay Bridge.

FADE TO BLACK.

MUSIC: Four The Moment's song, *AFRICVILLE*.[3]

CREDIT ROLL.

1992

Notes

1. Africville residents received electricity but few other municipal services.
2. Deed abandoning claim to a property.
3. Four the Moment, a female, Nova Scotian, *a capella* quartet, performs songs about oppression and resistance. "Africville" (1987), recorded by the group, was composed by group leader Delvina Bernard and poet-lyricist George Elliott Clarke. Both Bernard and Clarke appear in this anthology.

Peter A. Bliss Bailey
1953-

I dedicate these poems to Stella May Gibson and Rochella Paris.

Peter Bailey, 1991

Dedications
This book is dedicated to my blood and the dripping of my mind to the gutter for the sake of unworthy human beings.

I dedicate this book to Judas who rules the earth and to Jesus Christ who lost it.

I dedicate this book to every black child, woman and man in hope that we will continue to struggle.

I dedicate this book to all that take the time to read it and try to understand themselves.

I dedicate this book to my mother who has seen so much more than I. I'd like to express a great gratitude and respect to her.

I dedicate this book to someone I love but no longer have the strength to.

1975

To My Unborn Son

To my unborn son
I give these few simple
words of wisdom

Always be just what your
mind tells you to be

Listen to your heart
but never let it smother you

Cry when you feel the need
but never cry one single tear
in vain

Never listen to words form the wind
for they will surely deceive you

To you my unborn son I give
a very deep love

But you must find your own
strength and peace on earth

To you my unborn son,
I give you life

And all its torments
life and all its joy

And I pray you deal with it
better than your

father.

                                        1975

The Twilight Hour

I wrote one thousand words
and thought ten thousand thoughts

I have traveled mountains, valleys
and rivers for years

To find one single answer

What a fool to write so much
and think so long

What a fool to fail
for beauty

Never quite knowing the answer
never quite knowing the truth

what a fool to wait for
the final disappointment.

                                        1975

Old

Tramping
tramping
tramping

Through the snow

I have grown wise
and bear my scars
of life with pride and dignity

Yet I have not grown
wise enough

FIRE ON THE WATER

To hold on to one single
thing that I love.

                                                          1975

My Ebony Queen

She held me between her
warm black thighs

At times
when the snow cold
world outside

Tried to destroy my faith

She gave me strength enough
to face the cold and sleet

She gave me strength
to fight

She grew my seed
inside her womb
and suffered such
great pain

She tried so hard to build
me up and help
me see the way

Oh my Ebony Queen
I had to go away

I lost your love
I lost our child
I had to go away

Oh my Ebony Queen
I had to go away

I had to go away.

                                                           1975

Oh Africa

Oh Africa — The white man he did bleed you

Oh Africa — Your flesh and riches he did take

Oh Africa — He fucked you then he left you

Oh Africa — Independence he did give you

PETER A. BLISS BAILEY

Oh Africa — Revolution you must make

Oh Africa — The rich Black man he did deceive you

Oh Africa — His head you must now take

Oh Africa — Your children they will save you

Oh Africa — You will live for your children's sake.

1978

Oh Canada

Oh Canada!
you can keep your ugly winters
and your 40 belows

You can keep your salty street
and snow, they only
rot and ruin my cothes

You can keep your English bigots!

And your dumb Frenchmen too!

You can keep your hypocritical fascists politicians
I don't want the corrupt immoral dogs and their goons

You can keep your Montreal
with its psychopathic murdering criminals,
putrid air,
incompetent city officials.

You can keep your Toronto
 with its sterility, staleness
and racist western guard.[1]

You can keep your Calgary
with its pot-bellied bankers
that have their heads stuck
up a cow's ass hole

You can keep your Vancouver
with its dope peddling freaks
and rain

Oh Canada!
I will not stand on guard
for thee

FIRE ON THE WATER

You treat your native Blacks
and Indians like they have leprosy
or some other bad disease

Give me my shanty town in
Jamaica, Barbados, Trinidad, or Tobago

At least I won't die of frost bite,
air pollution or radiation poisoning.

1978

Ghetto Control

Groping Black faces
peering through windows

Searching the streets
for something to see

Or to imagine they've seen

Gottingen Street[2]
walked on by thousands
of Black feet

Walking back and forth
to and fro

They make their way
 to the white merchants' stores

Second-class citizens
in their own country

Their money goes to the
Greeks, Armenians and Syrians

So they they can buy their sons cars
and turn the business over to them
so that they can continue to perpetuate
the exploitation of the Black community

While the Black youth
must hang out on the street corners

Getting high
and wishing upon a star

A star
that never falls
on
Maynard

PETER A. BLISS BAILEY

Creighton
or Uniacke Square[3]

Police harassment at night
for the Black youth

Fine homes in the suburbs
fine private clubs at night
are what the youth of the shop owners
have to look forward to

And the sisters
they flow up and down the streets
Oh so beautiful

With babies so sweet
and a man who is not to be found
Until maybe, perhaps, possibly
on welfare day

Oh beautiful Black brothers and sisters
your existence appears to be like
that of a cow's cud

Chewed up and spit out
never changing

Just chewed up
and spit out

By a force
that you are either unable
or unwilling
to control

Ghetto control.

1978

Won't You Tell Me Where You're Going To

Where are you going
my young Black brother

Won't you tell me
where you're going to

Are you going to the Streets
to fight yourself a battle

When the war was lost
before the beginning of your life

FIRE ON THE WATER

Where are you going
my young Black sister

Won't you tell me
where you're going to

Are you going to the streets
to seek your fame and fortune
or to become an old woman
before your time

Where are you going
Oh my dear Black people

Won't you tell me
where you're going to

Are you going to the streets
with words of Jesus
to die like Martin[4]

Or do you care
where you're going to

Don't you think
we could at least
save the children

If there be no hope
for us

Oh my dear Black people
won't you tell me
where you're going to?

1978

Black Woman

You looked at me
a slave
you thought me to be
less a man than he
in all of his whiteness
A chance from you
I could not get
But I still love you
I ran to you from
chains of frustration
not knowing what to do
I did not care for

white lace
I did not care for jewels
I did not mean to hurt you so
Oh Lord, I was a fool
Black woman in all your
loving beauty
believe I only
have love and respect for you
could you ever fogive me
for only with you
could life be worth living
Black woman,
I love you.

1978

Notes
1. A racist organization active in Canada in the late 1970s.
2. A central street in Halifax and a main artery for the Black community.
3. Maynard Street, Creighton Street, and Uniacke Square in Haifax are associated with the Black Community.
4. Rev. Dr. Martin Luther King, Jr. (1929-1968), leader of nonviolent campaign for civil rights for African-Americans. Won Nobel Peace Prize in 1964. Assassinated April 4, 1968.

Faith Nolan
1957-

Africville

What happened to Africville?[1]
What happened to Africville?

Now I met a woman who spent her life working there;
Now that Africville's gone, she's in a highrise somewhere.
Out a highrise windows, I see her face;
She was so out of view, she was out of place.

What happened to Africville?
What happened to Africville?

Joey's in Toronto; family left him.
Daughter's gone insane;
can't make it.
Oh, left that community,
now they're on their own.
And it's so cold up here when you're on your own.

What happened to Africville?
What happened to Africville?

All the people just torn from the land,
Left alone without family or friends.
The pure water ain't by their side;
They've got to find someplace to hide.

What happened to Africville?
What happened to Africville?

A bulldozer in sixty-nine
tore it down; bad times—
All the people scattered.
It turned cold as ice.
You know the government,
it just ain't so nice.

What happened to Africville?
What happened to Africville?

1986

FAITH NOLAN

Edith Clayton [2]

In Nova Scotia, Sister Clayton weaves
So much beauty for us to see,
Weaving baskets like her mother before,
Weave on, sister, weave on.

Chorus
Weave on, Sister Clayton,
Stop the war, stop the hating,
Weave on, sister, weave on.

She weaves a basket for all the children
So they can grow in a world without hurtin',
Full of love and harmony,
Weave on, sister, weave on.

She weaves one basket for Hammonds Plains,
for Preston and the New Road gang;
She weaves one for all our people,
so long divided, so long apart.

She weaves one basket for you and me,
for us to stay together in unity.
The possibilities if we stand together
to make the world a better place.
We've been put down too long,
We're part of the human race.

In Nova Scotia, Sister Clayton weaves
so much beauty for us to see,
Weaving baskets like her mother before,
Weave on, sister, weave on.

1986

Marie Joseph Angelique [3]

Marie Joseph Angelique
Marie Joseph Angelique

I was talkin to my spirit and my spirit said to me,
Did you hear tell of Marie,
A sister born in slavery,
refused to be a slave, you see.
She said, My soul is my own for no man to keep.

FIRE ON THE WATER

She ran away from the home
she could never call her own
to burn Mount Royal down.
She lit her torch of freedom
and set the building on fire.
She said, If I can't be free,
I will burn in the mire.

Slave owners took her to the jail cell
and whipped her body;
then marched her through the town
for the wicked to see;
then they burned her at the town square.
I heard her screams.

My soul is my own
for no man to keep.

                                            1986

Torturer

The unspoken wars waged against children and women silently continue alongside the wars of inhumanity and dictatorships.

He broke Sherry's nose, ribs, and jaw,
He used a tire iron and crowbar.
Her kids were left alone a week,
Everybody knows, nobody speaks...

Where does the torturer live?

A gash in your jaw, teeth marks on your neck,
A weekend visit with Daddy, just like all the rest.
Black stockings cover your legs and arms,
you're lying for your Daddy one more time again...

Where does the torturer live?

The Children's Aid took them,
Mother meant no harm,
a burn on the little girl's chest,
a burn on the other girl's arm...

Where does the torturer live?

FAITH NOLAN

Husbands beating wives—
they think marriage gives them the right.
Too afraid of the bossman,
Women's screams ease their lives...

Where does the torturer live?

Pinochet[4] in Chile,
death squads in El Salvador,
while we're talking 'bout human rights,
let's take a look next door...

Where does the torturer live?

If only you'd come forward,
Behind closed lives and doors you hide.
Soon the doors will open,
We'll see then who's inside...

Tell me, where does the torturer live?

1989

Anna Mae Aquash[5]

My small offering of solidarity to Anna Mae, who gave her life in the battle of Native Indian peoples to retain their land and culture.

Like a hundred years before,
you want the native way of life.
Like a hundred years before,
Red woman dead in a freedom fight.

Thrown in a ditch,
covered in snow,
F.B.I. hid your body,
so your people wouldn't know.

Anna Mae Aquash,
Anna Mae Aquash.

They destroy your culture
as they steal your land.
To cover up their crimes,
they even stole your hands.

FIRE ON THE WATER

Oh Anna Mae,
the sound of your name
tells the story of no glory,
of this country's shame.

Where are your hands?
Anna Mae Aquash,
Anna Mae Aquash.

Here's the story of the people
who lay dead in their graves
from genocide, and massacre,
from a big fur trade...

Anna Mae, where are your hands?
Anna Mae, where are your hands?

From the Canadian Prairies,
where your Mama gave you life,
To the U.S.A.,
a murdered mother and wife.

                                                        1989

Aleticia

This companera (friend) and I would laugh when the pain was too great for tears.

Companera, companera
Aleticia, are you laughing?
Aleticia, are you laughing?

I miss those crazy days we'd dance,
laugh and love, pretend romance.
   Oh how we'd laugh.

You'd tell me of your mom and dad,
Detroit streets that left you sad.

Fourteen with no food to eat,
Sold yourself on the streets.

Money talked and bullshit walked,
Getting high, getting away was our only thought.

Oh Aleticia, are you laughing now?

FAITH NOLAN

How lucky to have left it all—
Now we live to tell such tales.

Oh Aleticia, are you laughing now?

I hear you're on the Texas border,
Back with your people writing the stories.

Companera, companera

Do you see the deportees?
Penny wages in factories.
Dying people all around.
Oh hold your ground.

I write about what I've seen,
I think of your laugh and where we've been—

Companera, companera
Aleticia.

1989

Freedom to Love

The state has no right to determine through laws which adults may love each other.

Laying with you at night,
you turn out the lights;
you wanna roll away from me,
you feel our love ain't right.

What I want is the freedom to love.

Sneaking and lying,
running and hiding,
we could give up, but
we've got to keep trying...

Not allowed in places,
and I can't love who I please;
you tell me who I have to love
and I call that slavery...

FIRE ON THE WATER

Blues done got me burning in my soul.
Blues done got me
and I don't know where to go.

Walking in the park,
swimming in the sea,
kiss you under water,
so nobody can see...

Hold your hand
on a sunny day,
kiss you in the airport
when you've been away...

Don't wanna be in the dark,
wanna turn on the light.
wanna love you, baby,
I know our love is right.

                                                        1989

Jellyroll

A blues expression of sensuality.

Well, if the world's alright, I must be wrong,
Cause I could jellyroll all day long.

Mama told me my jelly wasn't right,
but it feels so good, makes my life.

Jellyroll'n'jellyroll'n'jellyroll'n'jellyroll'n...

Upside down or rightside up,
any which way till I get enough.

If it feels good, do it night and day,
Helps you be happy, laughing all the way.

Morning, evening, afternoon delight,
Sweet tasting jellyroll makes my life.

Jellyroll'n'jellyroll'n'jellyroll'n'jellyroll'n...

                                                        1989

FAITH NOLAN

I Black Woman

I wrote this song to say that I will fight against the racist/sexist ways we as Black women are forced to live.

I Black woman can barely dance;
I'd rather read a book than jive or prance.
I hate wild parties and cheap romance;
I'm a woman on my own, taking my own stance.

I Black woman will not be used.

Don't call me brown sugar or sweet-time gal,
Talk like that don't give my heart a whirl.
I'm not hot in bed, it ain't my scene,
I am not part of your make-believe schemes.

I've seen mama beaten up by strange men;
sister's on the street turning tricks for them.
brother's out pimping and talking jive.
I saw daddy die drunk—couldn't make this life.

Don't call me your mama, your sister, your girl,
Don't call me anything in your fantasy world.
I ain't voodoo queen, an African dream,
I'm my own woman with my own damn scene.

1989

Notes

1. Africville, originally called Campbell Road Settlement, was a Black village which nestled on the shores of Bedford Basin in north end Halifax. Founded in 1815, it was bulldozed by the City of Halifax in the late 1960s and its residents relocated.
2. Edith Irene (Drummond) Clayton (1920-1989), a native of East Preston, was an internationally acclaimed East Preston basket weaver. In recognition of her artistry, she was awarded a medal by Her Majesty Queen Elizabeth II in 1977.
3. Marie Joseph Angelique, a slave, set fire to the house of her owner, Mme. François de Francheville, in April, 1734, thereby incinerating a portion of Montreal, Quebec. Angelique was imprisoned and hanged.
4. General Augusto Ugarte Pinochet (1915-), a Chilean army officer, led a bloody coup that resulted in the death of the popularly elected President Salvador Allende in September, 1973. Pinochet ruled Chile until democracy was restored in 1989.
5. Anna Mae Pictou Aquash (1945-1976) was a Micmac from Shubenacadie who became a Native activist. After receiving alleged death threats from an agent for the U.S. Federal Bureau of Investigation (FBI), Aquash was found, dead, in a South Dakota ditch in February 1976. Exposure was first ruled the cause of death. The FBI requested that her hands be cut off and then buried her as "Jane Doe." After her family learned that the dead woman was Aquash, a second autopsy revealed that she had been shot in the back of the head.

Delvina E. Bernard
1958-

I Love You Woman

we're here, standing at the shoreline
made it through some hard times
Black mother, Black daughter
made it through some hard times
Black mother, Black daughter

I see reflections of a past staring at me
of hard work, and women kneeling to pray
from the dusk, to the dawn
each day hard, each day long
giving me, my claim
I love you woman

we're here, standing at the shoreline
made it through some hard times
Black mother, Black daughter
made it through some hard times
Black mother, Black daughter

I see waters of east shores wearing you grey....
of tides white.... but never wearing you down
with your will, by your might
you have kept, gifts of old
giving me, my strength
I love you woman

we're here, standing at the shoreline
made it through some hard times
Black mother, Black daughter
made it through some hard times
Black mother, Black daughter

from the weakest one, to the strongest one
if we can say, who's weak and who's strong
the wisdom you've given....our blending as women
to conquer that troubled road
from your heart, by your life

DELVINA E. BERNARD

you have said, be we bold
giving me, my name
I love you woman

I'm a woman Black, and a woman first
cause I know what I have to meet
fire and thunder...waters of courage
are the gifts you've given to me

we stand as women
for the cause that needs assistance
against the wrong that needs resistance
we're still standing
we're still standing
standing
standing
standing

we're here, standing at the shoreline
made it through some hard times
Black mother, Black daughter
made it through some hard times
Black mother, Black daughter

1986

We Women

we women—Black, Beige, and Brown
have loaded-up...slave ships, ox carts...........and guns,

we have walked through fire, returned from sinking sand
chopped wood, moved stone, fetched water, as women still we stand

we've cast lines to our sisters....yellow, white, and red
stained with blood of witches, voodoo queens, and heretics

we wrote the symphony, that makes the white man sing
we wrote the blues......bebop, jazz, and swing
we wrote the lullaby, when massa's baby cried
we wrote the negro spiritual......each time a Black man died

Sojourner,[1] Harriet,[2] Ida,[3].................Zora Neale Hurston[4]
Rose Fortune,[5] Edith,[6] Portia,[7]................Lydia Jackson[8]

FIRE ON THE WATER

with tartan-tainted kente[9]
we've tugged and tried, and spun
200 years of women
and wove them into one

                                                  1992

Take Me to the Waters

baptized in the waters of old rivers
that flow through time
from Africa to Nova Scotian shores
on rock I stand all other ground
is sinking sand
take me to the waters
make me whole

take me to the waters
take me to the waters
take me to the waters
to be baptized

baptized in the name of the children in South Africa [10]
I pledge to fight freedom in their hand
baptized in the name of the children in Halifax
I pledge to fight for justice where I stand

take me to the waters
take me to the waters
take me to the waters
to be baptized

as sister of all nations take back the night
my faith in women's wisdom wages strong
our rising hymn spans race, and, tongue and religion
each of us as one, still each of own

take me to the waters
take me to the waters
take me to the waters
to be baptized

baptized in the name of sons
whose fathers struggled for my rights
whose mothers are my mothers
great and grand

DELVINA E. BERNARD

beside me not before me
shall we walk through fire
and drink from springs of life
woman to man.

take me to the waters
take me to the waters
take me to the waters
to be baptized

as sure as, the sun will cross the sky
and rest, to rise again
as sure as, maple leaves as red as blood do fall
praying hands shall open to receive the sword
the meek of tongue, shall shout the stone walls down.[11]

take me to the waters
take me to the waters
take me to the waters
to be baptized

1992

Lullaby for Cole Harbour[12]

the buses are driving the children away
one more daughter gone to school
gone to learn her place
each night at dusk a mother hums
and sings between her sighs
knowing that no lullaby
can hold pain inside

and how can she stop—
the tears about to fall
knowing that another child's innocence is lost
and how can she start—to teach African ways
when buses are driving the children away

the buses are taking the young men away
one more son sold down the river
gone to be a slave
just five years old, can't even read
yet he knows 'colour bar'
they've closed his school and bused him out
and now they'll close his mind

FIRE ON THE WATER

and how can she stop—
the tears about to fall
knowing that another child's innocence is lost
and how can she start—to teach African ways
when buses are driving the children away

how can a girl child know her worth?
how can she learn to stand?
how can a Black boy know his gifts?
how can he be a man?
when cultures are erased from time
for slates chalked full of lies
learning they are second class
not learning who they are

and how can she stop—
the tears about to fall
knowing that another child's innocence is lost
and how can she start—to teach African ways
when buses are driving the children away

1992

U.I.[13] *Line*

sun nips at my window 6:45
black coffee and a cigarette, the classified
skip a meal that I ain't got
I've gotta be on time
I don't wanna miss my spot
in that U.I. line.

cut backs and more tax
than we can pay
we've got layoffs, high mortgage
and interest rates
I've got lots of bills
but ain't got no income
I grab a five or a ten
from my family and friends
until my U.I. comes

cause we got no jobs here.....got no jobs here
it's a national affair........our home and native land ain't no
land of milk and honey........we true patriots
don't count a damn if we ain't got money!

DELVINA E. BERNARD

it looks like hard times, and bread lines
I can't pay my rent
by the time I pay food bills and utilities
my money's done spent
I've spent the last four years of my life
gett'n my degree
but I'm unemployed and depend'n on that U.I.C.

cause we got no jobs here.....got no jobs here
it's a national affair........our home and native land ain't no
land of milk and honey........we true patriots
don't count a damn if we ain't got money!

well, well, I got some mail the other day
'bout my U.I. claim
it hit me hard when I did find
the rules have changed
no cheque or no computer card
could I find
so I'm mov'n from the U.I.
to the welfare line

cause we got no jobs here.....got no jobs here
it's a national affair........our home and native land ain't no
land of milk and honey........and we true patriots
don't count a damn if we ain't got...money!...money!...money!

1986

Inkululeko Iyeza

it's amazing Lord, how salvation always comes
so late for most, but too soon for some
by and by, the burdens that we bear
will take wings in flight, as we lay down to rest

twenty six days and twenty six nights
heaven hurled down fire
thunder clapped, as scorn rained down on Pretoria[14]
children called out Stephen's name[15]..........*Inkululeko Iyeza*[16]
cold black blood bickered in my brain........*Inkululeko Iyeza*

it's amazing Lord, how salvation always comes
so late for most, but too soon for some
by and by, the burdens that we bear
will take wings in flight, as we lay down to rest

FIRE ON THE WATER

cuffs on flesh and flesh on stone
black freedom kept in chains
butchers hide behind apartheid laws to cover evil schemes
no denying they were lying...................*Inkululeko Iyeza*
judge and jury harmonizing...................*Inkululeko Iyeza*

*it's amazing Lord, how salvation always comes
so late for most, but too soon for some
by and by, the burdens that we bear
will take wings in flight, as we lay down to rest*

*Inkululeko Iyeza
Inkululeko Iyeza
Inkululeko Iyeza*

1986

Freedom Has Beckoned

*I won't let the world turn my head around
I won't let the world turn my head around
I won't let the world turn my head around
cause freedom has beckoned me to come*

I won't stop until the weak become the strong
I won't stop until the weak become the strong
I won't stop until the weak become the strong
cause freedom has beckoned me to come

And we won't be free
until the humble women speak!
and we won't be free
until the humble women speak!

*oh I won't ....
I won't let the world turn my head around
I won't let the world turn my head around
I won't let the world turn my head around
cause freedom has beckoned me to come*

I won't stop until Black people stand as one
I won't stop until Black people stand as one
I won't stop until Black people stand as one
cause freedom has beckoned me to come

and we won't be free
until South Africa is free!
and we won't be free
until South Africa is free!

oh I won't ....
I won't let the world turn my head around
I won't let the world turn my head around
I won't let the world turn my head around
cause freedom has beckoned me to come

I won't stop until the Pentagon has fallen
I won't stop until the Pentagon has fallen
I won't stop until the Pentagon has fallen
like Jericho its walls come tumbling down [17]

And we won't be free
until the trumpet sounds for peace
and we won't be free
until the trumpet sounds for peace

oh I won't ......
I won't let the world turn my head around
I won't let the world turn my head around
I won't let the world turn my head around
cause freedom has beckoned me to come

1986

Notes

1. Sojourner Truth (1797-1883), a U.S. preacher, seer, and teacher. Though illiterate, she was a powerful orator who crusaded against slavery and campaigned for women's rights.
2. Harriet Tubman (c.1821-1913), an escaped slave, returned 19 times to the South to lead more than 300 slaves to freedom.
3. Ida Bell Wells-Barnett (1862-1931), a journalist, led an anti-lynching crusade in the U.S. in the 1890s. She argued that lynching stemmed from a fear of economic competition.
4. Zora Neale Hurston (1891-1931), a novelist, author of *Their Eyes Were Watching God* (1937).
5. Rose Fortune lived in Annapolis Royal, Nova Scotia, in the 1880s. She was the first policewoman in North America and operated her own baggage service.
6. Edith Irene (Drummond) Clayton (1920-1989), of East Preston, was an internationally acclaimed basket weaver. In recognition of her artistry, she was awarded a medal by Queen Elizabeth II in 1977.
7. Portia White (1911-1968), of Truro, was a contralto and music teacher. Debuted at New York's Town Hall in 1944; gave Command Performance before Queen Elizabeth II in 1964. Famed for her *bel canto* technique, she sang in

FIRE ON THE WATER

English, French, German, and Spanish, and recited both spirituals and classical songs.

8. Lydia Jackson came to Nova Scotia in 1783 with the Black Loyalists. She was indentured for life (in effect, enslaved) to the household of a Dr. Bulman by whom she became pregnant. Bulman beat her so severely that she miscarried. In 1792, Lydia Jackson embarked for Sierra Leone, West Africa.

9. In Ghana, a long garment made from banded material loosely draped on or worn around the shoulders and waist.

10. The White minority population practised strictly enforced racial segregation (apartheid) and discrimination against the Black majority, 1948-1991; Blacks still cannot vote.

11. Joshua 6:5.

12. Cole Harbour High School, the largest in Nova Scotia, is attended by Blacks bused from Preston and Cherrybrook.

13. Unemployment Insurance.

14. Capitol of South Africa.

15. Stephen Bantu Biko (1946-1977) fostered the Black Consciousness Movement in South Africa. Arrested by South African police on August 18, 1977, he was kept naked and manacled and was probably beaten. After 26 days of this torture, he died from brain damage on September 12, 1977.

16. Zulu: Freedom is coming.

17. Joshua 6:4-5.

David Woods
1959-

Native Song
   (*For Cyril & Rosella Fraser*)

We find ourselves in purpose steeped,
To wrestle pain from these tired hands,
And erect new hope in the dark
horizon,
Beyond the reach of those who command.

A racist man's tools—
His education, his erudite words,
Have kept us closed,
We are not relieved by ecstatic
devotion to God,
Or by easy wish,
Despite all involvements
An agonized cry still emits from the soul.

Old men and old women
Know of the horror of those days,
When young and dressed in Sunday-fine,
They made their way to town,
And were fixed contemptuously
by white eyes—
Hounded from dust till dawn
Till their hopes were crushed,
And their sense of freedom died.
And drunk remembrances of old men
Of old days and old glories,
Or Mom Suse,[1] Pearleen Oliver[2]
that type,
Whose love rose like a sun
through the miasmal haze.

Yet as we wander in bowed status,
In minds estranged from themselves,
Dance as we always dance
In the old hall, or late-night club
What song shall rise from the

FIRE ON THE WATER

throat?
What great task will seize the hands?

And if that Preston[3] man in inspired
vision
Had not set about to construct
his itinerant church,
Or Mrs. Best[4]—awakened by study—
Asserted her womanly pride,
Or that Jones[5] man not considered and
meant his violence,
What would we be then?
Cadavers arranged like logs
Moving along a stink river
Not ours
but blowing on—lost forever.

An acrid mist rises above the land,
The sad breath of mother earth,
Tired of having weaned children
in deep cradles of human love:
Lucasville, Sunnyville, North Preston,
Weymouth Falls,
Children who are abandoned
And are left sad without choice.

I will go on my way
With a clear conviction,
To break these Nova Scotian
chains
So that a girl can decide
in a real way
To seize the earth by storm,
Or to sit back quietly into
the bosom of earth,
Nurtured by a long and ancient
love.
And I will fight—as wickedly
as the devil fights,
All that stifles her breath.

And when the sun settles
like a tired eyelid—
On the failed promise of Preston,
And ghosts of old appear,
I will sing a song

DAVID WOODS

And that song will be beautiful,
And that song will be great,
And no man on earth will be able
to block it from his ears.
And this will be my monument
Collected from the beauty and
pain,
Of all those who have lived
and died
In the hungry chambers
of the black dream.

1990

Harvey Barton at the Tavern

Harvey Barton goes to the tavern,
Sixty-five years old but still
held by its pulse,
Tap shoes on his feet—
Long, ridiculous scarf,
Alcoholic regret in his veins,
He is excited—it shows on
his face,
This place still gives him the spark
for living.

He has come here countless
times before,
First as a young man from
the country—
Handsome to a fault,
Now bald, arthritic—
He no longer cares for display,
He has his passion for dancing
Most else has faded away.

The stage is set—
His name is called,
And there is an old girlfriend Trudy
And there is a cousin—Rob,
Tap! Tap! The feet begin
The untalented beating upon
Life's huge drum.

FIRE ON THE WATER

He is a little ridiculous
But that does not matter,
His dance is understood
by all those gathered,
From the sturdy labourers
of Hammonds Plains,
To the young hookers
from "the Square,"[6]
His feet tell their tales
Of simple lives gone wrong,
Of wasted beauty and ruined
families
Of the simple and the poor—
Lost in an uncaring community.

He stays too long
And there is a bit of a fuss,
From someone who is perhaps too bitter,
Someone who is perhaps a little drunk,
But he is given applause
And flattered by kisses,
And what else—I ask
can we offer
To someone reaching his journey's end?
But to give him the stage—Amid a gathering of friends.
Shower him with applause—
Before the performance ends.

1990

For "Pixie" Beals

After a while—
Tired of dragging herself
through low-paying jobs
and dusty streets,
Tired of dead-end lovers
and burnt-out dreams,
Pixie picks up and
moves to Montreal—
In angered admission—
"Place can't do nothing
for me,
Got to go, get out of
here,
Men are bums."

Got to watch it though—
Actors often re-arrange
the scene
When the piece isn't working,
Bigger cast, more elaborate setting,
Still, the girl who wanders blindly onto the
stage,
With no rehearsed lines, no real talent
Remains consistent
The lost is the lost!

1990

Elsie Dorrington

Elsie Dorrington—
Never had it on her mind,
She was just another girl
in the twelfth grade
With a cute smile and
sprouting breasts.

But she got tired of the way
people kept looking at her,
Tired of the stupid things friends could
and did say,
Tired of "Nigger" on the walls
And insults in the halls.

And so she did this terrible, terrible thing,
—to keep her soft mind
—to protect her young heart
—to keep the tears from her eyes,
Started this street-walking, hand-slapping,
loud-talking thing,
Put on these tight, tight pants—
And became exactly as they said.

Now everybody's talking about
how bad Elsie Dorrington is,
"But she used to be so nice,"
I hear them say.
But I wonder if they ever
got tired
(Of being nobody when you really are somebody)
I mean real tired?

1990

FIRE ON THE WATER

Melda's Blues

She romanticized her yearnings—
Yet the freedom she found
in dance
Could not be repeated in the
grimy corners of reality.

Her romance, for example,
Could not stop her daddy from leaving,
The white man from refusing to rent,
Or her sister Lucie from becoming
a whore.

    1990

Love

"I love that girl so much
My hair getting kinkier"

    1990

Exclamation

Oh Lord! Oh Lord!
My little Mary had a baby!
Oh Lord! Oh Lord!
She went an done it —
Fore she turn a lady!

    1990

Report

Mary and Darren
Was both so ugly,
The reverend refused to
marry them,
On the grounds that
it wouldn't be fair
to their children.

    1990

DAVID WOODS

Rufus Peters

Rufus Peters
got Mrs. Saunder's 15 year old
pregnant,
Despite being married
and a respected deacon
in the Church.
Well "Ole Ruf" denied,
denied and denied
But nine months later
Them spacey teeth
On Missie's child,
Sure proved that deacon
had lied.

                                        1990

Signs

She blamed it on stomach flu,
But nine months later—
Everybody knew!

                                        1990

My Father

My father read the Bible
Each night before he
went to bed,
Then he would down a
shot of whisky
That kicked like a donkey
through his head.
And to this day
No word of a lie,
No one's sure if it's the religion
or the whisky,
Keeping that old man alive.

                                        1990

141

FIRE ON THE WATER

Aunt Viola

Aunt Viola wore lovely dresses
And spoke in a cultured tongue,
And she owned a house in the suburbs,
And smiled politely at everyone.
But get Aunt Viola up home on
the weekend —
And let a little liquor free her tongue.
Next thing you know Aunt Viola's
On the kitchen table —
Shouting and doing the bump!

1990

The Reverend

They accused the Reverend
of drinking up the Church
cheap wine,
Then they accused him of
messin' with the congregation
women,
When they finally accused him
of stealing from the Church
Building Fund,
The Reverend got mad and
burned the Church down!

1990

Hallelujah Dave

Hallelujah Dave is pure misery
in church,
Cause he makes more noise
than any church service is worth.
When the Reverend takes the pulpit
And is just about to start
Hallelujah jumps from his seat and hollers:
"Lord, on your mark!"
And before the Reverend can say
a second word
Hallelujah shouts at the top of his lungs:
"Praise the Lord!"
And when the Reverend's almost finished

DAVID WOODS

Just about to reach the end
Hallelujah's up with a big "Amen!"

1990

White Folks

White folks go to church
Can't even get 'em to smile,
Coloured folks go to church
You can hear 'em holler for miles!

1990

Epitaph

My friend Kipoch
Kenyan born,
Black as coal
From the Akamba tribe,
Has won an award —
and is off to New York,
After years of effort
He has begun to fly.

He is a riser in our
little town,
He is on the board of this
He is on the board of that,
He has appeared on local
television,
He is known among politicians.

Kipoch has vision
And it disturbs him day by day,
He must succeed!
He must succeed!
He is strict in his manner
He works slavishly,
He has improved his English
He has earned two degrees.

He is from Ikutha village
In Kenya's east,
His people are diseased and
strife-torn,
But he will not talk of that

FIRE ON THE WATER

now
He no longer writes to his
family,
He can no longer bear discussion
of his country.

Kipoch makes speeches
Whenever given a chance,
Among whites — he is known
to produce tears,
He does his native dances
For their amusement,
At night he is restless
and possessed by fear.

When black people in
the North-end began to
uprise,
Kipoch was quick to reproach:
"The world is ruled by a new
order of men:
The educated, the diligent,
One should not be fooled
by these lazy people
Or cloud the mind with
racial sympathies."

When a group of refugees
washed up along the shore,
Kipoch was even more
severe:
"These men are the jetsam
of troubled spots,
To allow them in the country
is to inherit their lowly woes,
And corrupt all we have achieved here."

I see him in a halo
of gold,
Standing in a brightened
ceremony,
Receiving applause from those
Who consider him extraordinary.

He will be standing there.
("Tucked" in tuxedo
Fixed in smile)
Standing there trembling and alone.

Once slavery took 15 million
men and women,
Raped and tortured their souls,
Kipoch is a modern type
He goes and serves willingly.

1990

Notes
1. Mrs. Susanna Smith (1883-1988), popularly knows as "Mom Suse," was born in Cherrybrook but lived most of her life in North Preston. She was lauded as the oldest resident in Halifax County in 1986.
2. Dr. Pearleen Oliver (1917-), of Lower Sackville, is a noted historian. Her work appears in this anthology.
3. Rev. Richard Preston (c.1791-1861), an escaped slave from Virginia, organized the African United Baptist Association (AUBA) of Nova Scotia in 1854 at Granville Mountain.
4. Dr. Carrie M. Best (1903-), of New Glasgow, is a noted historian. Her work appears in this anthology.
5. Burnley A. ("Rocky") Jones (1941-) of Halifax is a noted political activist and attorney.
6. Uniacke Square, a public housing development in North End Halifax.

George Elliott Clarke
1960-

The Sermon on the Atlantic

fishers float above
blue earth and death,
and lower lines insect-angels
ascend and descend, bringing
peace to priest amphibians,
slithering in a hungry world.
fishers let down these lines
to rescue those unwilling to be saved,
but who will greedily
seize the angled offer, and be yanked,
bleeding crimson froth at mad,
shocked-open mouths, now protesting
feverishly, upwards into heaven's
cold, blinding air.

1983

Campbell Road Church[1]

at Negro Point,[2] some forgot sleep
to catch the fire-and-brimstone sun
rise all gold-glory
over a turquoise harbour
of half-sunken, rusted ships
when it was easy to worship
Benin[3] bronze dawns,
to call "hosanna" to archangel gulls....
but none do now.
rather, an ancient CN[4] porter lusts for Africville,
beautiful Canaan[5] of stained glass and faith
made shacktown of shattered glass and shame,
rats rustling like a mayor's robe.
he rages to recall
the gutting death of his genealogy,
to protest his home's slaughter
by butcher bulldozers
and city planners molesting statistics.

at Negro Point, some forgot sleep,
sang "oh freedom over me,"
heard mournful trains cry like blizzards
along blue Bedford Basin...

none do now.

1982

Hammonds Plains African Baptist Church

drunk with light,
i think of maritime country.
i sing of Birchtown[6] blues, the stark,
sad beauty of that Kimmerian[7] land.
i dream of a dauntless dory
battling the blue, cruel combers
of a feral, runaway ocean—
a trotskyite[8] ocean in permanent revolution,
turning fluid ideas over and over
in its leviathan mind,
turning driftwood, drums, and conundrums
over and over...
then, crazy with righteous anger,
i think of Lydia Jackson,[9]
slave madonna, soon-rich with child,
whose Nova Scotian owner,
distinguished Dr. Bulman,
kicked her hard in the stomach,
struck her viciously with fire tongs,
and then went out upon the ocean
in his dory
to commune with God.

1982

Crying the Beloved Country[10]

why can i not leave you
like a refugee?
reluctantly, i abandon
your sea-bound beauty,
shale arms and red clay lips
sipping fundy streams.
why can i not depart from you
like any proud, prodigal son,

ignoring your eyes'
black baptist churches?
what keeps me from easy going?
Mother, is it your death
i fear
or my life?

                                                        1983

Primitivism

he could not escape
the wilderness. bark
encrusted his wine bottles.
his pencils grew fur
and howled. sentences
became wild eagles that
flew predatory patterns,
swooping out of a white sky-
page to rip apart field
mice-images, scurrying
for meaning. a carcass-
manuscript rotted on a shelf
or a hillside. he could
not tell the difference.
a bear-trap of ideas
snared him: he could
not poeticize
the country
and not become it;
his poems filling with
neanderthal nudes,
prowling punctuation,
snarling sounds, guttural.

                                                        1983

Evangelist[11]

crows crack a white, porcelain sky
with one fine, black line;
through the fracture, some light
falls, filters, but little.
beneath that pale plate,
i was pressed, flattened,
made weary, the same as everyone,

my gospel-fire fainting.
then, i found a few believers, forest
boards, and raised a bonfire-church
in the name of God and the old songs
no other church would sing.
We dark ones joined,
becoming incendiary,
one vast conflagration unto God.

    1983

Christ Church
(To Septimus Clarke)

the holy mountains reverberate
with fish and lumber sale cries,
campaign promises, and glint
in sunlight and fog.
withdrawn now, awaiting
transport to my scourged nation again,
Shelley mine and joy,
the Africans of *Megumaage*[12] established
in Christ church, true church, Baptist church,
ablaze with spirit, each member
a pentecostal[13] flame, i see
rural chapels sparkling white, prayers requited.
no matter now, death or destiny,
i have other fires to bank.
i go. this record?
Go tell it on the mountain.
Go sound the Jubilee.

    1983

Weymouth Falls

walk within dusk's goldcopper
autumn, oh you, who art black
but comely, transfiguring nefertiti![14]
watch the jetjade of nightpines
become delicate, rippling hair
moondark as your own,
falling ebonblue velvet.
wonder what seeking lover
will discover your secret beauty,
opening its sacred book

FIRE ON THE WATER

to find illumination, what solomon[15]
found in egypt.

1983

salvation army blues

seeking after hard things—
muscular work or sweat-swagger action—
i rip wispy, Help Wanted ads,
dream of water-coloured sailors
pulling apart insect wings of maps,
stagger down saxophone blues avenues
where blackbirds cry for crumbs.
i yearn to be ulyssean,[16] to roam
foaming oceans or wrest
a wage from tough, mad adventure.
for now, i labour language,
earn a cigarette
for a poem, a coffee
for a straight answer,
and stumble, punch-drunk,
down these drawn and quartered streets,
tense hands manacled
to empty pockets.

1982

Whylah Falls

Preface

Founded in 1783 by African-American Loyalists seeking Liberty, Justice, and Beauty, Whylah Falls is a village in Jarvis County, Nova Scotia. Wrecked by country blues and warped by constant tears, it is a snowy, northern Mississippi, with blood spattered, not on magnolias, but on pines, lilacs, and wild roses.

1990

Look Homeward, Exile[17]

I can still see that soil crimsoned by butchered
Hog and imbrued with rye, lye, and homely
Spirituals everybody must know,

Still dream of folks who broke or cracked like shale:
Pushkin, who twisted his hands in boxing,
Marrocco, who ran girls like dogs and got stabbed,
Lavinia, her teeth decayed to black stumps,
Her lovemaking still in demand, spitting
Black phlegm — her pension after twenty towns,
And Toof, suckled on anger that no Baptist
Church could contain, who let wrinkled Eely
Seed her moist womb when she was just thirteen.
    And the tyrant sun that reared from barbed-wire
Spewed flame that charred the idiot crops
To Depression, and hurt my grandaddy
To bottle after bottle of sweet death,
His dreams beaten to one, tremendous pulp,
Until his heart seized, choked; his love gave out.
    But Beauty survived, secreted
In freight trains snorting in their pens, in babes
Whose faces were coal-black mirrors, in strange
Strummers who plucked Ghanaian banjos, hummed
Blind blues — precise, ornate, rich needlepoint,
In sermons scorched with sulphur and brimstone,
And in my love's dark, orient skin that smelled
Like orange peels and tasted like rum, good God!
    I remember my Creator in the old ways:[18]
I sit in taverns and stare at my fists;
I knead earth into bread, spell water into wine.
Still, nothing warms my wintry exile — neither
Prayers nor fine love, neither votes nor hard drink:
For nothing heals those saints felled in green beds,
Whose loves are smashed by just one word or glance
Or pain — a screw jammed in thick, straining wood.

                                                            1988

The River Pilgrim: A Letter[19]

    At eighteen, I thought the Sixhiboux wept.
Five years younger, you were lush, beautiful
Mystery; your limbs — scrolls of deep water.
Before your home, lost in roses, I swooned,
Drunken in the village of Whylah Falls,
And brought you apple blossoms you refused,
Wanting Hank Snow[20] woodsmoke blues and dried smelts,
Wanting some milljerk's dumb, unlettered love.
    That May, freights chimed xylophone tracks that rang
To Montreal. I scribbled postcard odes,

FIRE ON THE WATER

Painted *le fleuve Saint-Laurent comme la Seine*[21]—
Sad watercolours for Negro exiles
In France, and dreamt Paris white with lepers,
Soft cripples who finger pawns under elms,
Drink blurry into young debauchery,
Their glasses clear with Cointreau, rain, and tears.
    You hung the moon backwards, crooned crooked poems
That no voice could straighten, not even O
Who stroked guitars because he was going
To die with a bullet through his stomach.
Innocent, you curled among notes — petals
That scaled glissando from windows agape,
And remained in southwest Nova Scotia,
While I drifted, sad and tired, in the east.
    I have been gone four springs. This April, pale
Apple blossoms blizzard. The garden flutes
E-flats of lilacs, G-sharps of lilies.
Too many years, too many years, are past....
    Past the marble and pale flowers of Paris,
Past the broken, Cubist guitars of Arles,
Shelley, I am coming down through the narrows
Of the Sixhiboux River. I will write
Beforehand. Please, please come out to meet me.
                  As far as Beulah Beach.

                                        1989

The Wisdom of Shelley

You come down, after
five winters, X,
bristlin' with roses
and words words words,
brazen as brass.
Like a late blizzard,
You bust in our door,
talkin' April and snow and rain,
litterin' the table
with poems—
as if we could trust them!

I can't.
I heard pa tell ma
how much and much he
loved loved loved her
and I saw his fist

fall so gracefully
against her cheek,
she swooned.

Roses
got thorns.
And words
do lie.
I've seen love
die.

1990

The Argument

  Stars are bread crumbs. Selah Clemence wonders, "Is this all there is?" She stumbles, in a delicate drunk, a green path. The moon fidgets like a maniac. When she finds her bedroom, she places pine branches in her dresser to perfume her clothes that otherwise would smell of roses. Pablo Gabriel calls her "Gatito," Spanish for "little cat." She is that lithe. Queen Natchal. How could she be otherwise? She stages a pageant of colours — silver, crimson, and yellow — against the backdrop of her dark skin.
  She soaks in bright scents of *chypre*,[22] coconut, and honey so that she is consciously sweet. She indulges in such extravagant gestures as her hands nonchalantly stroking her voluptuous hair and other Romantic acts such as draping her red silk panties on the edge of a bathtub where a choice explorer can find them. A brash innocent, always she is dying for love of some no-count man who abandons her always after a month of epic scandals that forever brand him a bastard and the most miserable dog in Jarvis County.
  She is a modern martyr for love, bearing witness to its betrayal by men who fear their own nakedness. Thus, she has made alcohol her one true love. She has wedded liquor because men have betrayed her sexuality as they have betrayed their own. Public songs stolen from crackling radios, warped records, and tavern performances are her refuge, her dowry, her diary of hurt, her modernism, her lyric beauty already become tragic although she is only twenty-nine. When a camera squints upon her, it x-rays her flesh, discovering keyboards, guitar strings, and flute holes hidden in her bones. Selah is Beauty oppressed because of its perfection. She quotes Bessie Smith:[23]

    You can't trust nobody,
    You might as well be alone;
    Found my lost friend,
    And might as well stayed at home.

1990

FIRE ON THE WATER

Love Letter to an African Woman

Beloved:
In my miserable weakness, I disparage you; in my childish fear, I ignore you; in my profound self-hatred, I lash out at you; in my gross ignorance, I use you, abuse you, but then can't understand why I lose you. I am stupidly contradictory — rude, when I should be respectful; cold, when I should be caring.

I want you to obey me. Why won't you? I want you to be who I think you should be. Why are you so stubborn? To ask such questions is to confess that I have lost our history.

Are you not Sheba,[24] "black but comely," who enlightened Solomon; Nefertiti,[25] who brought glory to Egypt; Harriet Tubman,[26] who brandished a pistol and pledged to shoot any slave who tried to abandon her freedom train; Lydia Jackson,[27] who fled Nova Scotian chains to found Sierra Leone; Portia White,[28] who enthralled the world with song; Carrie Best,[29] who gave us a *Clarion* voice; Pearleen Oliver,[30] who brought our history on home; Marie Hamilton,[31] whose steadfast compassion has uplifted many? Are you not these heroines and a hundred more?

African daughter, forgive me my several trespasses. I have been so weak, so scared!

Black Queen, teach me to cherish children; teach me the pride of our Blackness, our Negritude; teach me that manhood is not the dumb flexing of muscles but the impassioned sharing of love in fighting injustice.

Let us make a pact, I will cease my fear; you will cease your despair.

Black Madonna! I love your African essence, your faith in children, your insatiable desire for freedom, your swift intelligence, your sharp passion, your secret strengths, your language that tells no lies, your fashion that is colour, your music that is gospel-lullaby, your lips like crimson berries, your skin like soft, moist night, your eyes like dusk, your hair like dark cotton, your scent like rich butter, your taste like raisins and dates and sweet wine.

Let us join. My love, let us join.

1987

Blues for X

Pretty boy, towel your tears,
And robe yourself in black.
Pretty boy, dry your tears,
You know I'm comin' back.

I'm your lavish lover
And I'm slavish in the sack.

Call me Sweet Potato,
Sweet Pea, or Sweety Pie,
There's sugar on my lips
And honey in my thighs.
Jos'phine Baker[32] bakes beans,
But I stew pigtails in rye.

My bones are guitar strings
And blues the chords you strum.
My bones are slender flutes
And blues the bars you hum.
You wanna stay my man,
Serve me whisky when I come.

                                          1990

In Acadian Jarvis County

I remember how Selah opened
like a complex flower.
I brushed her sleeping breasts
and they startled awake:
two, rippling fish.

She said my kisses on her breasts
were "bee stings and cool mist."
After words, I carried her, seared
with grass and kisses, from the river.

                                          1990

In the Field

Selah glares at me
   impatiently, not seeing
        the apple blossoms.

                                          1989

Translated from the Spanish

   Come, my love, come, this lonely, passionate,
Nova Scotian night. Your voice trembles like wings,
Your bones whisper. Under the moon, I stroll

FIRE ON THE WATER

The shadowed road, awaiting your dark eyes
And sandalled feet. My love, if I have to,
I will pace this blue town of white shadows
And black water all night, if I have to.

1990

On June 6th

   Othello stood with friends
amid lush, fiery leaves,
tested intricate white
lightning, writhing like sleek
vipers in cages of glass.
Had he dreamt his soon death,
He would have contemplated
carbon culture:
how skin and bones
become diamonds
after so much pain.
It is our fate
to become beautiful
only after tremendous pain.

1990

Eulogy

   His breath went emergency in his lungs,
His felled heart grasped impossibly at light;
A thrown bouquet, he dropped softly to earth.
Torn from sweet oxygen, O wilted fast.
   We have now come to bury our beloved.
We stumble through smoke, broken sentences,
Snatch fresh, pale lilies from his dark bier,
Watch water smash its white brains on black rocks.
   Children, all deaths concentrate in this one.
The rain now falling is each, single tear.

1990

Notes
1. Established in 1849 in Campbell Road Settlement, the early name for Africville. The church, renamed Seaview United Baptist Church, was bulldozed in the middle of the night by the City of Halifax during the Africville Relocation of the 1960s.

2. A spit of land at the Narrows where Halifax Harbour joins Bedford Basin. It was part of the Black Refugee community of Africville, which, founded in 1815, was bulldozed by the City of Halifax in the late 1960s and its residents relocated.
3. A Republic in west central Africa, independent since 1960. Its Edo and Yoruba peoples are renowned for their skill in bronze casting.
4. Canadian National Railway.
5. The Promised Land.
6. A Black Loyalist settlement near Shelburne.
7. Kimmeria, a mythical, shrouded land far across the seas.
8. Leon Trotsky (1879-1940), a Russian revolutionary and Bolshevik leader. His theory of "permanent revolution" led him into conflict with Josef Stalin. Expelled from the Soviet Union in 1929, he was murdered in Mexico by Stalin's agents in 1940.
9. Lydia Jackson came to Nova Scotia in 1783 with the Black Loyalists. She was indentured for life (in effect, enslaved) to the household of a Dr. Bulman by whom she became pregnant. Bulman beat her so severely that she miscarried. In 1792, with 1,200 other Black Loyalists, Lydia Jackson embarked for Sierra Leone, West Africa.
10. Cf. Alan Paton, *Cry, the Beloved Country* (New York: Scribner, 1948).
11. Rev. Richard Preston (c.1791-1861), an escaped slave from Virginia, organized the African United Baptist Association (AUBA) of Nova Scotia in 1854 at Granville Mountain. He was assisted by Septimus Clarke (d. 1859), first secretary of the AUBA. This poem and the next are written in Preston's persona.
12. Micmac name for Nova Scotia.
13. Acts 2:1-4.
14. xiv century B.C. (Eighteenth Dynasty) Egyptian queen.
15. x century B.C. king of Israel, noted for his wisdom. He married a pharaoh's daughter (I Kings 3:1). The Song of Solomon, a love duet between Solomon and his bride, is probably about their wedding.
16. In Greek legend, Ulysses (Latin name for Odysseus), king of Ithaca, wandered the seas for ten years, experiencing many adventures, after the fall of Troy.
17. Cf. Thomas Wolfe, *Look Homeward, Angel* (New York: Scribner, 1929).
18. Ecclesiastes 12:1.
19. Cf. Ezra Pound, "The River Merchant's Wife: A Letter," in *Cathay* (London, 1915), a book of Chinese verse translations.
20. Clarence Eugene "Hank" Snow (1914-), born in Liverpool, is a father of Canadian country and western music.
21. I... / Painted the St. Lawrence River [in Quebec] like the Seine River [in France].
22. A heavy perfume made from sandalwood.
23. Bessie Smith (1894-1937), the U.S. "Empress of the Blues," was the greatest of the classical singers.
24. The Queen of Sheba visited Solomon to test his wisdom. See I Kings 10:1-13. In the ancient Ethiopian book, the *Kebra Negast* or *Glory of Kings*, Sheba is an Ethiopian sovereign named Makeda who returns from Israel bearing Solomon's son, David. He later became the first king of Ethiopia, Menelik I.
25. See note 14.
26. Harriet Tubman (c. 1821-1913), an escaped slave, returned nineteen times to the South to lead more than 300 slaves to freedom.
27. See note 9.
28. Portia White (1911-1968) of Truro was a contralto and music teacher. Debuted at New York's Town Hall in 1944; gave Command Performance before Queen Elizabeth II in 1964. Famed for her *bel canto* technique, she sang in four languages, recited both spirituals and classical songs.

29. Dr. Carrie M. Best (1903-), of New Glasgow, published and edited *The Clarion*, an Africadian newspaper. Her work appears in this anthology.
30. Dr. Pearleen Oliver (1917-), of Lower Sackville, is a noted historian. Her work appears in this anthology.
31. Dr. Marie Hamilton (1912-), of Halifax, a teacher and community worker. She is the mother of Sylvia Hamilton, whose work appears in this anthology.
32. Josephine Baker (1906-74), U.S.-born singer, dancer, and actress, became a sensation in France after emigrating there in 1925. Lauded as a performer and as a member of the Resistance during the Nazi occupation of France (1940-1944).

Floyd Kane
1970-

Letter: Woman to Man

I love you. And I mean it.

Lately, I have found myself standing in front of the immaculate mirror your parents gave us as a wedding gift, wondering about the status of my life in yours. This is a hard statement to fathom but I'm sure you can understand. Anyway, standing in front of this mirror, I look at myself and I search for—to coin a phrase—"that girl who used to be me." Where is she? Dead, I suppose, replaced by a woman who was never quite sure of what she wanted out of life. Dammit. I just spilled ashes on the paper. I guess I should stop smoking but...But anyway, I have to finish this and there is much that you have to understand.

There are certain things I knew—from day one—that I didn't want in my life; certain things I did. Nothing special, just things that women tend to expect, nowadays. A little respect, some compassion, a morsel of love. I know things have been tough and that you've been having hard times but I have to ask myself, "How long do you starve, Sheila? How long do you wait for the man you married to show himself again?" I'm sure by now that you know the time's up.

Knowing you, Rog, this is probably the last place you'd look. The kitchen, a woman's domain. Knowing you, these words might languish on the page for a week before you acknowledge them. Acknowledge. What a word.

I have never done anything this hard in my entire life, it's like asking me to jump from a chair with a rope tied around my neck. And I can't breathe now. I'm kicking up hell trying to get this noose from around my throat but I can't. It's as if dying is the only way to be free of you. And yes, that is what this is all about: freedom. I would go to bed at night and I would watch you as you slept. So contented. So goddamned proud of your pain and I'd catch a flash of my blackened eye in that mirror and I just wanted to scream. I was good though, I stopped myself, for fear that you'd hit me again: harder, this time.

You were, and as far as I know, always will be the one person who drives me to emotional extremes. Two seconds of joy, one second of pain. One second of joy, one second of pain. One second of joy, two seconds of pain. It has been like a game with you lately, "Let's see how we can ruin Sheila's complacency." Christ, Roger. I would give the world not to have to write this letter. To be able to rip it to shreds and fall into your arms when you get home at 6:05 tonight. But it just cannot be. I refuse to be hit again, I refuse to be suspicious and timid around the one person I've been completely naked with.

I'm crying here, do you realize this? Everyday for the past ten weeks, I have found myself going into fits of tears because of you. I could be doing the laundry or vacuuming the floor and all of a sudden this feeling swept over me—like it is now. It felt like anger, but it wasn't.

It wasn't sorrow or pain or any of those things that I should feel. It's hard to describe. A cool, a funeral chill, that brings me these jagged images of me lying in a hole with someone shovelling dirt in my face. It chokes me. It is bitter and I can't move, I can't talk, I can't scream. So I cry. It's all I can do. It is all that I can do, now.

I'm not leaving because my honey complexion has been turned bluish or because I hate having to wash the blood from the bath towels. I'm leaving because no broken bone, no pitch-black bruise, could ever hurt me the way watching you turn into a stranger has. At night, when I lay beside you and you touch me. Touch me with the same hands that have brutalized me. I'm being touched by a stranger. It is a stranger who pulls me close to him, kissing me, making me wish that I had a means of slitting his throat. Being raped by a stranger could never compare with this.

The truth is that I find myself beginning to make excuses for your changes. I'm not tidy enough. The food is a bit overdone. He's had a hard day, it's not his fault. He just can't help himself. You know, there were times that I saw you coming a mile away and I just stood there, telling myself, "He married me, he pays the bills, if he's frustrated, if he needs a punching bag, let it be me. I owe it to him." This is how I was beginning to think and it frightened me. So while you were at work, I went out and found a job. It's not as good as yours and my lifestyle will change drastically, but it's a start. I rented a bachelor apartment too—this is not just a moment of passion on my part; it isn't Crichton Park,[1] but once again, it's a start. The invitation to your staff Christmas party is on the nightstand beside the bed. Tell them I'm sick if you like; it wouldn't be a lie, entirely. Sick because I've been forced to give up someone who is as much me as myself.

Jesus, I didn't realize that time had passed so suddenly, what was supposed to be ten sentences has become a novel. Guess who's the villain? (I'm grinning.) I'm sorry, Roger, even at a time like this I can't be vindictive. I've taken everything that rightfully is mine. Not that I have room or need for a lot of it. The Probe—God, I love that car—that you brought me last year for Christmas—what a surprise!—will remain with me and I will make the payments. The crystal unicorn that you brought back from your trip to Switzerland—every time that I look at it I think of how delicate everything is, how illusory. Where are these words coming from? A heart that has not shown itself in a great many months? Maybe.

Lastly, Roger, I'd like to thank you for doing the "honourable" thing and marrying me. Maybe because of that decision we were destined to come to this. I would like to believe that we made one another happy, at least for a little while. Remember how we wept in unison over the still form of our infant. If only I could get *that* man back. These past few months, it has been like watching talc turn to sand, sand turn to granite, granite to diamond. I loved—love—you, you bastard. You're in my heart and I just hate myself, despise myself, for letting this happen. You don't know how much of me is still floating in this room. You don't know the void that you've left in my heart: the emptiness.

Maybe now, you will understand things and find yourself as I have. Only problem is, if you were to find yourself—not even a second—after reading this letter, it still wouldn't save you and me.

Good-bye, Roger, maybe alone we can find the happiness that I always thought—wrongly, I suppose—that we could find together.

Love. I mean it.

Sheila

1992

Note

1. A residential subdivision in Dartmouth.

Selah:
Envoy

The editor's mother, Geraldine Elizabeth Clarke (nee Johnson), at age 19, at home in Three Mile Plains, Nova Scotia, in April 1958.

Lives

William Lloyd Clarke (1935-) was born in Halifax. While a youth, he was an apprentice to a sign painter and later studied at the Nova Scotia College of Art and Design. A learned man and an aficianado of classical music, Clarke, the father of George, lives in Dartmouth. His painting, *Moonscape*, appears on the cover of *Volume 1 and 2*.

Raymond L. Parker (1936-) was born in Granville Ferry. Parker attended Annapolis Regional Academy, but left school at 16. He drove trucks for the Lewis Transfer company, a Black-owned firm, for 24 years. A singer, songwriter, and musician, Parker has performed with such groups as The Rockin' Drifters, The Ambassadors, The Country Ramblers, and the Rhythm Four and Countrytones, earning the tag, "The Charley Pride of Nova Scotia." In the early 1970s, he wrote a play, "Beyond the Dark Horizon." In 1987, the Black Cultural Centre published a novella version. In 1988, Charles R. Saunders adapted the novella for a CBC radio script. Parker lives in Lequille.

Frederick Ward (1937-) was born in Kansas City, Missouri. He studied art at the University of Kansas and music at the University of Missouri. After working as a Hollywood songwriter, Ward went to New Mexico and began to write. In 1970, Ward wound up in Halifax because of a dock strike. His books include the novels *Riverlisp* (1974), *Nobody Called Me Mine* (1977), and *A Room Full of Balloons* (1981), and *The Curing Berry* (1984), a collection of poems. Also a composer, actor, playwright, and screenwright, Ward has won many awards, including "Best Actor," presented by the Chicago International Film Festival for his role in a National Film Board feature he wrote, *Train of Dreams* (1987). Ward lives in Montreal and Blockhouse, N.S.

Alfreda Smith (1939-) was born in North Preston. As an infant, she was so ill she was not expected to live. However, she believes that God answered her parents' prayers that her life be spared. Smith states, "I came over on the Lord's side at the age of eleven. And started to teach Sunday school at the age of twelve." Smith has studied child evangelism, piano, musical theory, and health care. She has also studied child care and development. Smith lives in North Preston.

Walter Borden (1942-) was born in New Glasgow. He attended Acadia University and the Nova Scotia Teachers' College, from which he graduated in 1964. He taught for three years before moving to New York City to study acting. Returning to Halifax in the 1970s, Borden plunged into acting, writing, and community work. He has appeared in over fifty plays, including Molière's *Tartuffe* (as Tartuffe) at Neptune Theatre and George Boyd's "Gideon's Blues" at Upstart Theatre. Borden has performed his one-man show, "Tightrope Time" (1986), from Vancouver to Amsterdam. In 1989, he was awarded the Outstanding Theatre Achievement Award (1989) by the Nova Scotia Drama League. A brother of George, Borden lives in Halifax.

Frank S. Boyd (1943-) was born in Halifax. Boyd earned a B.A. from Saint Mary's University in 1969, a M.A. from Dalhousie University in 1975, and a B.J. from the University of King's College in 1981. A specialist in public relations and communications and a social researcher and analyst, Boyd has worked with such agencies as the Canadian Labour Congress, the Retail Council of Canada, the Black United Front, and was director of the Black Cultural Centre. In 1976, he annotated and republished Peter McKerrow's *Brief History of the Coloured Baptists of Nova Scotia, 1783-1895* [1895]. He has also authored numerous essays and articles. A brother to George, Boyd lives in Elmsdale.

Charles R. Saunders (1946-) was born in Elizabeth, Pennsylvania. He holds a B.A. in psychology (1968) from Lincoln University. He emigrated to Canada in 1970. A freelance writer, Saunders has published three Africanist, fantasy-genre, popular novels: *Imaro* (1981), *Imaro II: The Quest for Cush* (1984), *Imaro III: The Trail of Bohu* (1985). Two of his screenplays—*Amazons* (1987) and *Stormquest* (1988)—have become feature films. Saunders has also written a radio play—*The Sam Langford Story* (1987). His non-fiction credits include, "Africville: From the Outside In," (1989) and *Sweat and Soul: the Saga of Black Boxers* (1990). Saunders lives in Halifax, where he is a popular columnist with *The Daily News*.

Gloria Anne Wesley-Desmond (1948-) was born in Yarmouth. She attended the Nova Scotia Teachers' College, graduating in 1970. A teacher, Wesley-Desmond published her first book of poems, *To My Someday Child,* in 1975. Her work has appeared in such historic Black Canadian anthologies as *Canada in us now* (1976) and *Other Voices* (1985). Wesley-Desmond lives in Monastery.

Maxine Tynes (1949-) was born in Dartmouth and has lived there all of her life. While a student at Dalhousie University, she won the Dennis Memorial Poetry Prize in 1974. An English teacher at Cole Harbour High School and a former, freelance broadcaster with CBC Radio, Tynes's first book of poems, *Borrowed Beauty* (1987), won her the People's Poet of Canada Award in 1988. *Woman Talking Woman,* her second book of poems, appeared in 1990. Also that year, the

Dartmouth Public Library opened the Maxine Tynes Room. In 1991, CBC aired a television version of her short story, "In Service." Tynes is the first Africadian to be appointed a member of the Board of Governors of Dalhousie University.

Sylvia Hamilton (1950-) was born in Beechville. She attended Acadia University, graduating with a B.A. in English and Sociology. She has published poetry and articles on Africadian history in several journals. Hamilton researched, wrote, and co-directed *Black Mother, Black Daughter*, an award-winning documentary produced by the National Film Board of Canada in 1989. She has worked with such organizations as the Voice of Women and the National Congress of Black Women. A former radio journalist, Hamilton has held various posts within the Department of Secretary of State, including acting Regional Director for Nova Scotia. Hamilton lives in Halifax.

George Boyd (1952-) was born in Halifax. He attended Saint Mary's University and the Nova Scotia Institute of Technology, from which he graduated in 1976. A journalist, he has written numerous magazine and broadcast pieces. In 1989, he won an Atlantic Journalism Award for a radio documentary. He has written two plays—"Shine Boy" (produced by Neptune Theatre in 1988) and "Gideon's Blues" (produced by Upstart Theatre in 1990)—and two screenplays--"Consecrated Ground" (1990) and "Sweet Train Gonna Come" (1991). Boyd is also host of CBC Morning News, broadcast simultaneously on CBC and CBC Newsworld. He plans to found a theatre company called the Canadian Black Theatre Society. Boyd lives in Halifax.

Peter A. Bliss Bailey (1953-) was born in Halifax and with his parents moved at the age of nine to Montreal. There, he attended Dawson College and, in 1975, published his first book of poetry, *This is my song*. In 1976, Bailey returned to Nova Scotia and took up a position with the Black United Front. His mature experiences inspired a suite of poems, "Halifax Sketches," which appears in his second book of poems, *Going Black Home* (1978), also published in Montreal, where he had returned in 1977. In 1982, Bailey formed a Black performance poetry quartet, "The New Life Poets," which consisted of two poets and two musicians. Bailey still lives in Montreal, where he continues to write. He is a child care worker for disturbed children and youths.

Faith Nolan (1957-) was born in Halifax but raised in Toronto. The daughter of Cape Breton parents who were both musicians, Nolan is a singer, composer, a guitarist whose songs are strongly rooted in the cultural language of Black North American music: spirituals, gospel, jazz, and blues. Educated in threatre, opera, and writing, her lyrics voice concern for the world of the common people. She has released three albums: *Africville* (1986), *Sistership* (1987)—both issued by Multicultural Women In Concert, and *Freedom to Love* (1990), issued by Aural Records. Nolan lives in Toronto but remains closely tied to her Nova Scotian ancestry.

Delvina Bernard (1958-) was born in Halifax and grew up in Lake Loon and Cherrybrook. She graduated from Saint Mary's University with a Bachelor of Commerce degree in 1982. In 1981, Bernard helped to found the *a capella* quartet, *Four the Moment*, which performs songs about Black history, women's history, Third World struggles, and human rights. In 1988, Bernard produced the group's first album, *We're Still Standing*, which won several award nominations. Her song, "Freedom Has Beckoned," was included on the CBS Much Music *Soul in the City* compilation album. And Bernard wrote the music for Sylvia Hamilton's 1990 film, *Black Mother, Black Daughter*. Bernard lives in Halifax.

David Woods (1959-) was born in Trinidad but emigrated with his family to Nova Scotia in 1972, settling in Dartmouth. He attended Dalhousie University briefly before leaving to pursue a career as a community organizer and artist/writer. Woods has worked as Program Director for the Black Cultural Centre and founded the Cultural Awareness Youth Group. Under his leadership, the organization was awarded the Commonwealth Youth Service Award in 1986. A playwright, poet, painter, actor, organizer, and filmmaker, Woods has staged many plays, including his own "For Elsie Dorrington" (1983), and appeared in films. His first book of poems, *Native Song*, was published in 1990. He lives in Halifax.

George Elliott Clarke (1960-). See "About the Editor."

Floyd Kane (1970-) was born in Halifax and grew up in East Preston, where he still lives. He began to write seriously while a student at Cole Harbour High School. He published his first story, "The Mistake," in Grade 12. Kane then wrote a play, "Black Money," for the Black Cultural Centre. He has since written articles. He states that "The page acts like a mirror; be it mystery, romance, adventure, every word on the page offers the reader a glimpse into the writer's persona." Kane is an English student at Saint Mary's University.

FIRE ON THE WATER

Errata for Volume One
(The following biographies were omitted from Volume One)

Rev. John Marrant (1755-1791) was born, free, in New York. However, he grew up in the South. Rather than learn a trade, he studied violin and French horn for two years. At the age of 13, he became a Christian. Opposed by his family for his faith, he lived a while among the Cherokees. Following the American "trouble," Marrant was ordained a minister in an evangelical sect. He voyaged to Nova Scotia in 1785 to preach to the Black Loyalists, and organized a congregation at Birchtown. In 1789, Marrant left for England, where he died in 1791. His *A narrative of the Lord's wonderful dealings with John Marrant, a black*, which appeared in London in 1785, received at least 21 printings.

William Riley (c. 1856-1943), of Cherrybrook, was a prime source of Black folk songs for Nova Scotian song collector Helen Creighton, who interviewed him extensively in 1942 and 1943. In one of their conversations, he informed her that his mother was part Scotch and white, while his paternal grandfather was half-Spanish and half-French. He seems to have been a composer and *raconteur*. Creighton offers transcriptions of several songs sung by Riley in her book, *Traditional Songs from Nova Scotia* (1950), and in her article, "Collecting Songs of Nova Scotia Blacks," which appears in *Folklore Studies in Honour of Herbert Halpert* (1980).

Arthur Huff Fauset (1899-1983), a pioneer African-American anthropologist and educator, was born in Flemington, New Jersey. He attended the University of Pennsylvania, where he earned his B.A., M.A., and Ph.D. degrees. Fauset visited Nova Scotia in 1925 and released *Folklore from Nova Scotia* in 1931. His books include a biography of Sojourner Truth (*Sojourner Truth*, 1938) and his classic study of urban Black religion, *Black Gods of the Metropolis* (1974; 1976).

Raymond L. Parker

Frederick Ward

Alfreda E. Smith

Walter Borden

Frank S. Boyd
(Photo Mick McManaman)

Charles R. Saunders

Maxine Tynes
(Photo Shirley Robb)

Sylvia Hamilton
(Photo Henry Bishop)

George Boyd
(Photo John R. Davis. from
Halifax Faces, Café Books, 1989)

Peter Bliss Bailey

Faith Nolan
(Photo Joyce Hinton,
Encore Productions)

Delvina E. Bernard
(Photo Alex Murchison)

David Woods
(Photo George Georgakakos)

George Elliott Clarke
(Photo Andrews-Newton
of Ottawa)

Floyd Kane

Acknowledgements

For permission to reprint the selections in this book, thanks are due Dr. Frances Henry (for several spirituals—"That Great Day," "When the Trumpet Sounds," "Hold Onto Jesus," "I Came to Jesus"— that she recorded and transcribed), Dr. Pearleen Oliver (for her own work and that of Rev. Dr. W.P. Oliver), the other writers and copyright holders whose works are represented, and the following publishers:

Afro-Nova Scotian Enterprises—for selections from *McKerrow: A Brief History of the Coloured Baptists of Nova Scotia—1783-1895*, 1976, by Peter E. McKerrow, edited by Frank Stanley Boyd, Jr.

American Folklore Society—for selections from *Folklore from Nova Scotia*, 1931, compiled by Arthur Huff Fauset. Note: These selections are not for further reproduction.

The Art Gallery, Mount Saint Vincent University; The Black Cultural Centre for Nova Scotia; the Africville Genealogical Society; The National Film Board, Atlantic Centre—for "A visit to Africville," 1989, by Charles R. Saunders.

Bilongo Publishers—for selections from *To My Someday Child*, 1975, by Gloria Wesley-Daye [now Gloria Wesley-Desmond].

The Black Cultural Centre for Nova Scotia—for selections from *Canaan Odyssey: A poetic account of the Black experience in North America*, 1988, by George A. Borden; for a selection from *Beyond the Dark Horizon*, 1987, by Raymond L. Parker; and for a selection from *Canada's Black Battalion: No. 2 Construction, 1916-1920*, 1986, by Calvin W. Ruck.

The Clarion Publishing Company Ltd.—for selections from *That Lonesome Road: The Autobiography of Carrie M. Best*, 1977, by Carrie M. Best.

McGraw-Hill Ryerson Limited—for "Cherry Tree Carol [A]" from *Traditional Songs from Nova Scotia*, 1987, by Helen Creighton and Doreen Senior.

Polestar Press—for selections from *Whylah Falls*, 1990, by George Elliott Clarke.

Pottersfield Press—for selections from *Saltwater Spirituals and Deeper Blues*, 1983, by George Elliott Clarke; for selections from *Borrowed Beauty*, 1987, and from *Woman Talking Woman*, 1990, both by Maxine Tynes; and for selections from *Native Song*, 1990, by David Woods.

Tundra Books—for "Purella Munificance" from *Riverlisp: Black Memories*, 1974, by Frederick Ward.

Williams-Wallace Publishers—for selections from *The Curing Berry*, 1983, by Frederick Ward.

About the Editor

George Elliott Clarke is the author of two books of poetry: *Saltwater Spirituals and Deeper Blues* (Porters Lake, N.S.: Pottersfield Press, 1983) and *Whylah Falls* (Winlaw, B.C.: Polestar Press, 1990). In 1981, he won First Prize for Adult Poetry in the annual competition sponsored by the Writers' Federation of Nova Scotia. In 1983, he was runner-up for the Bliss Carman Award for Poetry, given by the Banff Centre, School of Fine Arts. In 1991, he received the Archibald Lampman Award for Poetry, presented by the Ottawa Independent Writers. His poems have appeared in such magazines as *Descant, Quarry, The Idler, The Fiddlehead, Grain, Prism International, The New Quarterly, Callaloo (U.S.A.), Germination, Event,* and *TickleAce* and in such anthologies as *The Atlantic Anthology, Poets 88, Other Voices, Halifax: A Literary Portrait,* and *Choice Atlantic.* He has also written lyrics for the *a capella* folk-gospel quartet, Four the Moment.

Born in Windsor, Nova Scotia, Clarke grew up in North End Halifax, where he became a political and artistic activist. In 1979, he helped to establish the now-defunct Black Youth Organization of Nova Scotia. In 1985, he organized the Weymouth Falls Justice Committee to protest racism in the Nova Scotian justice system. From 1987 to 1991, he was an assistant to Howard McCurdy, MP, in Ottawa.

A scholar of English, Clarke holds an Honours B.A. degree from the University of Waterloo and a M.A. degree from Dalhousie University. He is presently a doctoral candidate at Queen's University.

A Note on the Type

Fire on the Water, Volumes One and Two, were typeset on data processing equipment, using Ventura Publishers software. Typography and page layout were executed by Elizabeth Eve.

The typeface is in New Century Schoolbook (Adobe), which is based on Century type invented by L B. Benton and T. L. De Vinne in 1894. Century Schoolbook was cut in 1926 for American Type founders.